THE UPPER ROOM

DAILY MEDITATIONS FROM AROUND THE WORLD

Sarah Wilke
Publisher

Carmen M. Gaud
Guest Editor

INTERDENOMINATIONAL
INTERNATIONAL
INTERRACIAL

77 EDITIONS
39 LANGUAGES

The Upper Room
January–April 2011
Edited by Susan Hibbins

The Upper Room © BRF 2011
The Bible Reading Fellowship
15 The Chambers, Vineyard, Abingdon OX14 3FE
Tel: 01865 319700; Fax: 01865 319701
Email: enquiries@brf.org.uk
Website: www.brf.org.uk
BRF is a Registered Charity

ISBN 978 1 84101 791 4

Acknowledgments
The New Revised Standard Version of the Bible, Anglicized Edition, copyright © 1989, 1995 by the Division of Christian Education of the National Council of the Churches of Christ in the USA. Used by permission. All rights reserved.

The Holy Bible, New International Version, copyright © 1973, 1978, 1984 by International Bible Society. Used by permission of Hodder & Stoughton Publishers, a member of the Hachette Livre UK Group. All rights reserved. 'NIV' is a registered trademark of International Bible Society. UK trademark number 1448790.

Extracts from the Authorised Version of the Bible (The King James Bible), the rights in which are vested in the Crown, are reproduced by permission of the Crown's Patentee, Cambridge University Press.

Scriptures quoted from the Good News Bible published by The Bible Societies/HarperCollins Publishers Ltd, UK © American Bible Society 1966, 1971, 1976, 1992, used by permission.

Printed in the UK by HSW Print.

The Upper Room: how to use this book

The Upper Room is ideal in helping us spend a quiet time with God each day. Each daily entry is based on a passage of scripture, and is followed by a meditation and prayer. Each person who contributes a meditation to the magazine seeks to relate their experience of God in a way that will help those who use The Upper Room every day.

Here are some guidelines to help you make best use of The Upper Room:

1. Read the passage of Scripture. It is a good idea to read it more than once, in order to have a fuller understanding of what it is about and what you can learn from it.
2. Read the meditation. How does it relate to your own experience? Can you identify with what the writer has outlined from their own experience or understanding?
3. Pray the written prayer. Think about how you can use it to relate to people you know, or situations that need your prayers today.
4. Think about the contributor who has written the meditation. Some Upper Room users include this person in their prayers for the day.
5. Meditate on the 'Thought for the Day', the 'Link2Life' and the 'Prayer Focus', perhaps using them again as the focus for prayer or direction for action.

Why is it important to have a daily quiet time? Many people will agree that it is the best way of keeping in touch every day with the God who sustains us, and who sends us out to do his will and show his love to the people we encounter each day. Meeting with God in this way reassures us of his presence with us, helps us to discern his will for us and makes us part of his worldwide family of Christian people through our prayers.

I hope that you will be encouraged as you use the magazine regularly as part of your daily devotions, and that God will richly bless you as you read his word and seek to learn more about him.

Susan Hibbins
UK Editor

In Times of/For Help with...

Below is a list of entries in this copy of *The Upper Room* relating to situations or emotions with which we may need help:

Anger: Apr 7

Anxiety: Feb 25, 28; Mar 15

Assurance: Mar 19

Bible reading: Jan 12, 21; Feb 2, 28; Mar 2, 14, 23, 28, Apr 1, 2, 12, 26

Change: Jan 22, 27, 31; Feb 16; Mar 10, 23; Apr 1, 9, 16, 20

Christian community: Jan 4, 9, 12, 31; Feb 13, 15; Mar 21, 25; Apr 1, 3, 8, 21

Compassion: Mar 21; Apr 6

Creation/Nature's beauty: Feb 2, 7, 2; Mar 11, 31; Apr 14, 18, 20, 28

Death/Grief: Jan 4, 28; Feb 16; Mar 8, 19; Apr 19

Decisions: Jan 14; Feb 4, 12

Doubt: Jan 24, 27

Evangelism: Apr 2, 8, 23, 24, 26

Failure/Disappointment: Jan 11, 13, 28; Feb 6, 17, 23; Mar 9, 10, 12; Apr 4, 10

Family: Mar 2, 8, 10, 14, 19; Apr 19

Finance: Feb 14; Mar 18, 24; Apr 1

Forgiveness: Jan 18, 23, 30; Feb 12; Mar 6, 21, 26; Apr 3, 5, 7, 15

Generosity: Jan 1, 15; Feb 9, 15, 19, 25

God's comfort: Jan 4; Feb 24

God's love: Jan 8; Feb 5, 22, 24, 27; Mar 1, 11, 21; Apr 14, 22

God's presence: Jan 5, 24, 26, 27, 31; Mar 3; Apr 14

God's provision: Jan 28; Feb 4, 18, 19, 20; Mar 9, 17, 31

God's will: Mar 24, 25; Apr 1, 29

Growth: Mar 3, 14; Apr 18, 20, 25, 28

Guidance: Jan 11, 14, 16, 20, 31; Feb 4; Mar 16, 20; Apr 1, 12

Guilt: Jan 30

Healing/Illness: Jan 4, 9, 13; Feb 28; Mar 19, 20; Apr 23

Hospitality: Apr 9

Job concerns: Jan 5, 27, 31; Feb 11, 20, 25; Mar 13; Apr 1, 29

Living our faith: Jan 2, 8, 12; Feb 3, 13, 16 17; Mar 2, 8, 15, 16, 22; Apr 4, 17

Loneliness: Mar 29

Loss: Jan 4, 22; Mar 23, Apr 1, 19, 29

Materialism: Feb 9, 14; Mar 18, 24

Mission: Jan 2, 15, 16, 19; Feb 15, 21, 25; Mar 4, 20, 27; Apr 2, 6, 16, 21, 26

New beginnings: Jan 6, 9, 11, 18, 30; Feb 23; Mar 6, 10; Apr 5, 24

Obedience: Feb 4, 23; Mar 5, 10, 15, 16, 28

Parenting: Jan 8, 12, 13, 20, 22, 23; Feb 3, 6, 10, 18, 24, 28; Apr 3, 22

Patience: Mar 15

Peace/Unrest: Jan 11, 14; Feb 4, 14, 28; Mar 15; Apr 4, 29

Prayer: Jan 5, 9, 14, 26, 31; Feb 2, 8, 11, 16, 23; Mar 2, 4, 14, 15; Apr 1, 19, 29

Salvation: Jan 6, 23, 30; Mar 10, 26; Apr 5, 10, 11, 15, 22, 23, 25

Self-confidence: Jan 3, 6; Feb 1

Serving: Jan 15, 16, 19; Feb 1, 21; Mar 5, 13, 16, 20, 24, 27; Apr 1, 6, 16, 21, 30

Social issues: Apr 6, 15

Sharing faith: Jan 2, 8, 10, 20; Feb 13; Mar 8, 22, Apr 2, 4, 16, 17, 24, 26

Spiritual gifts: Jan 3; Mar 5; Apr 8

Spiritual practices: Jan 21, 22; Feb 8; Mar 2, 4, 9, 14, 15, 23, 28; Apr 18, 29

Stewardship: Jan 1, 15; Feb 9, 25; Mar 5, 31; Apr 8

Stress: Jan 7, 25, 31; Feb 11, 20, 23, 26

Tolerance: Apr 5, 6, 15

Trust: Feb 11, 18, 22, 26, 27; Apr 1

Worry: Feb 14, 24; Mar 15, 24; Apr 1, 7

'Pray without ceasing' (1 Thessalonians 5:17).

Pastor Hugo Urcola, the distributor of El Aposento Alto (the Spanish edition of The Upper Room) in Argentina, was puzzled when Maria said to him, 'I believe we are Methodists.' Hugo went on to find out that Maria worked on a farm whose owner was a Methodist woman. She gave copies of El Aposento Alto to Maria, who read it with her husband. Little by little Maria's neighbours learned of their reading and wanted to join them, and a group began to read the Bible and study the meditations together.

This story reminded me of the life of the Christian community after Pentecost (Acts 2:46–47). There were no denominations, no budget assigned, no ordained pastors. People, convinced that something special had happened, simply gathered to learn more. They were committed to the resurrected Christ and interested in growing in their faith together. The Christians practised simple things: learning from the apostles, eating meals, praying and worshipping together, and sharing all they had with 'glad and sincere hearts'.

Consider the tremendous impact of this ancient community: from their simple practices, the Christian church grew. In the book On Our Way, Dorothy Bass suggests that to live a whole life we need to live 'attentively... together, in the real world... for the good of all... in response to God' (Upper Room Books, 2010, p. 8). For centuries Christians in many lands have rediscovered that we need to encourage all these practices in order to live fully as God's children.

Hugo's story represents the power of The Upper Room. It is a small magazine with a simple format. But the meditations, Bible readings and reflections can have a profound effect. Simple practices that nurtured people's faith in Jerusalem and in the Argentinean pampas can do the same for us today.

Carmen M. Gaud
International Editor, El Aposento Alto

The Editor writes...

We watched the birds as they visited the feeders and bird baths in our garden, hoping to see a family of colourful goldfinches which sometimes flitted in and out, rarely staying long but bringing with them a welcome flash of red and gold against the cold whiteness of the snow and the grey sky. The temperature was barely above freezing, and the birds were busy stocking up for an even colder night that lay ahead.

A small bird alighted on the feeding tray. 'Only a sparrow,' said my husband. I looked at it more closely. Beautiful gradations of glossy brown lay along its wing feathers, with darker dabs of colour on its head and breast. Maybe it is one of our more common garden birds; but it is a precious creation of God never the less.

I thought of Jesus' words about sparrows: 'Are not two sparrows sold for a penny? Yet not one of them will fall to the ground unperceived by your Father' (Matthew 10:29, NRSV). God's care for all his creation is summed up in that one sentence: even a tiny sparrow is cherished in the sight of the God who keeps the planets spinning in space. Nothing is so small that it is unworthy of his attention and love, nothing so insignificant that it does not reflect the glory of its Creator.

So what about us? Perhaps we too sometimes feel small and unnoticed by the crowd. In the world's eyes, we may feel we do not amount to much. But God does not look at us in the way the world does; as his children, we are loved beyond measure. We can take comfort from Jesus' next reassurance: 'And even the hairs of your head are all counted. So do not be afraid; you are of more value than many sparrows' (10:30–31).

Susan Hibbins
Editor of the UK edition

PS: The Bible readings are selected with great care, and we urge you to include the suggested reading in your devotional time.

Giving to God

Read Matthew 22:15–22
God created humankind in his image.
Genesis 1:27 (NRSV)

The Pharisees tried to trap Jesus by asking him if it was lawful to pay taxes to the emperor, Caesar. Jesus' response was, 'Give… to the emperor the things that are the emperor's, and to God the things that are God's.' As I think about Jesus' words, I wonder, 'How do I go about giving to God the things that are rightfully God's?'

The widow in the Gospel story (Luke 21:1–4) was surrounded by people much richer than she—and they made sure others noticed them as they gave their gifts. Most of them gave out of their abundance, hardly knowing they had given anything. The widow gave two mites, tiny copper coins holding the least value in the Roman monetary system, but she gave all she had. Jesus said she had given more than all the others.

The money belonged to Caesar because it had his image on it. In a much more fundamental way, we belong to God because we have God's image on, and in, us. In order to give to God what belongs to God, we must, like the widow, give all we have: our very lives. When we give ourselves, God has all of us, including our money and our possessions. And like the widow, even the poorest person among us can give generously to God.

Prayer: *Dear Lord, help us to give ourselves and all that we have to you. Amen*

Thought for the day: Even the person with little can give much to God.

Nancy Evelyn Allen (Tennessee)

A Great Privilege

Read 2 Corinthians 5:16–21

We are ambassadors for Christ, since God is making his appeal through us.

2 Corinthians 5:20 (NRSV)

Recently I was walking through the block of flats where I live when one of the maintenance staff asked if I had a moment to talk. He said that he had been in my flat to repair something, and he noticed all the Christian books in my bookcase. 'Are you a Christian?' he asked.

'Yes,' I replied.

'Well,' he said, 'I would like to be one too.' This allowed me to talk with him about my faith in Christ.

The apostle Paul reminds us that we are ambassadors for Jesus Christ. That is not an option once we take the name 'Christian' for our identity. Everything we say, do and are can testify to what we believe. The question is whether that testimony is positive or negative. Does it draw others to Christ, or does it push them away?

Being a Christian is an awesome responsibility. However, it is also a great privilege to be able to talk about our faith to people who need and want a relationship with Christ.

Prayer: *Dear Lord Jesus, we are grateful for what you have done for us. Help us to share the good news of your saving love with others, by our words and our deeds. Amen*

Thought for the day: Each of us may be the first Christian that others meet.

Dick Ryley (New York)

Body Partners

Read 1 Corinthians 12:12–27

All [the body's] different parts have the same concern for one another. If one part… is praised, all the other parts share its happiness.
1 Corinthians 12:25–26 (GNB)

What an apt picture the apostle Paul gave us when he described believers as being parts of Christ's body! As with a human body, each of us has our own unique part to play. No one else can contribute what God has planned for you or me within Christ's own much-loved and valued body.

Lately, I have had to relearn this. In our church several gifted people younger than I make a fine contribution to the church's ministry. As I watch and listen, seeing the eager response people give them, my mind is filled with 'If-only-I-could-do-that' thoughts. It's easy to become resentful when instead I could be happy because God is at work through these other members of our common body. After all, when an athlete wins a race his whole body jumps with joy. You never see an arm or a leg resentfully refusing to share in the celebration.

So it's important for me to celebrate because God's work is being done so well by other parts of Christ's body. At the same time, it's important for me to identify my own unique place and responsibility in the body and to experience the pleasure of fitting in with everyone else as, united, we respond to Christ, our head.

Prayer: *Dear Lord, help each of us to find and fill our particular role, in love and loyalty to you. Amen*

Thought for the day: Each one of us can take joy in what all of us do for God.

Elaine M. Brown (Perthshire, Scotland)

Out of the Darkness

Read 2 Corinthians 1:3–7

What I say to you in the dark, tell in the light; and what you hear whispered, proclaim from the housetops.
Matthew 10:27 (NRSV)

I was left alone with two young sons when my husband of 25 years died from a blood disease. He had been firmly confident that God would heal him. So when I received the message from the hospital that he had died, I broke down. My life seemed to fade into total darkness.

But 'the God of all consolation, who consoles us in all our affliction' sent many friends to me, friends who had experienced the kind of sorrow that I was feeling. They said the right words and did the right things. Sometimes they only sat silently with me. These God-given friends made my life bearable. I learned that God uses people who have experienced pain and sorrow to console others whose despair is overwhelming them and robbing them of peace and joy.

When our heart is breaking, God meets us at the deepest level of our suffering and consoles us as only God can. And most often, God uses other people for this consoling work.

Prayer: *Dear God of mercy, help us to trust in you when pain overwhelms us. Teach us how to console others in the ways you console us. Amen*

Thought for the day: What we learn in the darkness, God will use to bring light.

Ingrid A. Rönnberg (Skåne, Sweden)

God's Presence

Read Isaiah 55:10–13
The heavens declare the glory of God; the skies proclaim the work of his hands. Day after day they pour forth speech; night after night they display knowledge.
Psalm 19:1–2 (NIV)

On some mornings I pray to be aware of God's presence throughout the day. When the day doesn't turn out quite as I anticipated, I may ask, 'God, where were you today?' Instead of feeling God's touch in the rain, I grumble about getting wet. Rather than hearing God's voice in a song, I complain about being stuck in traffic. Busy with my work, I fail to see God in the smile of the person I pass in a supermarket.

On days like these, I allow my hectic pace to keep me from recognising reminders that God provides throughout the day. God may have demonstrated awesome power in a morning thunderstorm. God may speak to me throughout the day in songs on the radio, an encouraging word from a friend, a greeting from a stranger. God's beauty may shine in the sunset. Goodnight kisses from my children always bring God's touch.

Signs like these are present every day. But when we look for only monumental wonders that signify the presence of God, we may miss the daily reminders God provides.

Prayer: *Thank you, God, for your constant presence. Make us more aware of you in every aspect of our lives. We pray as Jesus taught us, saying, 'Father, hallowed be your name, your kingdom come. Give us each day our daily bread. Forgive us our sins, for we also forgive everyone who sins against us. And lead us not into temptation.'* Amen

Thought for the day: I will keep my eyes open for small reminders of God's presence.

Marcia Hodge (Florida)

Clean Channels

Read John 7: 37–39
Do not quench the Spirit.
1 Thessalonians 5:19 (NRSV)

A blocked drain is never a thing of beauty; neither does it occur at a convenient time! With swirling scum going everywhere except down the drain, we were grateful when a neighbour came to our rescue. He lifted the manhole cover in the garden and pushed and twisted his drainage rods along the pipe work until he felt resistance. An extra thrust and a mighty rush of water came pouring through, bringing the offending cause of the blockage—a lump of grey sediment, built up, no doubt, over many months.

Being quiet before God one day, I had to confess that for years I had struggled with the unreasonable attitude of a fellow Christian toward me. Try as I might, I was defeated every time I had to deal with this person, and the hurt and humiliation I felt was marring my own Christian walk and witness. Suddenly God revealed to me that I was just like that blocked pipe—needing to be spiritually unblocked so that the Holy Spirit could flow unhindered through me to others. I asked for God's forgiveness and help, and I felt a sudden release from all antagonism. God had spiritually unblocked me!

The following Sunday the situation at church had not changed, but I had, and the Lord's joy flowed freely through me! Just as we must make sure our outside pipe does not silt up, so I must ask for daily cleansing from any residue of hurt and resentment that could so easily build into another 'blockage'.

Prayer: *Lord Jesus, make me a clean channel for you to use.*

Thought for the day: I will keep my heart free from the build-up of resentment and hurt feelings.

Jeanne Selley, Devon, England

Asking for Help

Read Matthew 14:22–33

Pride goes before destruction, a haughty spirit before a fall.
Proverbs 16:18 (NIV)

One winter day I took part in a cross-country ski lesson. As the group started skiing, I tried to push off as the instructor had shown us, only to slip and fall. I finally got going but was constantly slipping, sliding and falling down. I could not keep up with the group and quickly became frustrated, wet, cold and sore. Yet instead of asking for help, I got back up and tried again and again. Finally, the instructor noticed that I had fallen behind and came back to help me. He took one look at my skis and said, 'Here's your problem. These skis need to be waxed. Here, I have some wax with me.' After he had waxed my skis, I easily skied up to the rest of the group.

Later I asked myself, 'Why didn't you ask for help sooner?' I concluded that pride made me try to learn on my own. Yet because I had no experience I needed the instructor's help even to know what the problem was.

In my spiritual life, often I catch myself trying to do things on my own, without Christ's help, even though I know that Christ is always ready to help those willing to ask. In order to become the persons God created us to be and to live out the life we are called to, we need the help and guidance of Christ.

Prayer: *Dear Lord, grant us grace and humility so that we ask for your help in all that we do. May you be glorified through our efforts. Amen*

Thought for the day: God wants us to be humble and ask Christ for help.

Kristin Hammer Evans (Tennessee)

'See You at Home'

Read 1 John 4:7–16

Jesus… said, 'I am the light of the world. Whoever follows me will never walk in darkness but will have the light of life.'
John 8:12 (NIV)

My new stepfather asked my brother and me if we wanted to call him 'Dad' or 'Jim'. We immediately chose to call him 'Dad'. Either way, we would come to see that the commitment he made to us was like the unconditional commitment God has made to us.

When I played junior football, I searched the crowd for Dad. He always came to my games even though I did not always play. Afterwards, he would wait to talk to me before I got on the bus. Dad saw how disappointed I was in myself. His words have stayed with me: 'I will always be proud of you, whether you are the star player or you sit on the bench. I love you. See you at home.'

Isn't that similar to what our heavenly Father says to us? In Christ, God offered us a chance to call him 'Father', not because of what we do but because of who God is and wants to be in our lives. Because Dad followed Christ, I have seen Christ's light. The true light comes only from God, and I want to show my children that light. I want to tell others about Christ.

The Father looks forward to seeing us at home.

Prayer: *Dear God, show us how to reflect the light of Christ so that everyone we know sees your unconditional love. Amen*

Thought for the day: Even when we are disappointed in ourselves, God's love for us is constant.

Mark Brewer (Texas)

Praying in Need

Read James 5:13–18

Are any among you sick? They should call for the elders of the church and have them pray over them, anointing them with oil in the name of the Lord.

James 5:14 (NRSV)

Some years ago, our congregation began offering anointing with oil and prayers for healing for those in our community. At first people were hesitant to ask for prayer or to come forward to receive anointing for physical or emotional scars. But in time these healing services became very important to our congregation. Now it is not uncommon for dozens of people to seek healing and prayer.

We easily forget that all of us are broken people. Each of us has needs that may require God's healing touch or the support of a caring community. Indeed, great things happen when we open our lives to God's amazing grace. Consider your life today. Where are you in need? What prayers for yourself, your family, or for others do you need to offer?

Christianity is not a solitary faith for only the strong but a bond that calls us to pray for one another in our infirmities and our need. And often, in our weakness, we discover the strength of God.

Prayer: *Dear Lord, make us instruments of your peace and healing. Where we are weak, make us strong. Where we are wounded, heal us. In Jesus' name we pray. Amen*

Thought for the day: Through Christ's wounds we are healed.

Todd Outcalt (Indiana)

The Word of their Testimony

Read John 17:20–26

Jesus said, 'I made your name known to [those whom you gave me], and I will make it known, so that the love with which you have loved me may be in them, and I in them.'
John 17:26 (NRSV)

Each day as I read my Bible and this daily devotional magazine, the testimonies of my brothers and sisters in Christ bring me closer to God and to them. I walk with them through their daily experiences. I share their personal stories, their struggles to forgive, the anguish and the heartache they feel. I rejoice with those who rejoice in every triumph and victory. Because of their closeness to God, I feel that I touch God.

Just as those 120 believers mentioned in Acts 1:15 must have been close to one another as they waited and prayed, similarly I draw close, not only to God but also to my brothers and sisters all over the world as they share their experiences of God's love. I thank God for each one, and I am strengthened and encouraged by the faith and courage of their testimonies to live as God calls me to.

Prayer: *Thank you, Lord Jesus, that all those who believe are one in you. May our faith be strengthened each day as we talk with one another about what we learn of and do for you. Amen*

Thought for the day: The family God gives us goes beyond race, nation and time.

Link2Life: *Give a subscription to* The Upper Room *to someone today.*

Joan Lake (New South Wales, Australia)

Waddling into Danger

Read Matthew 7:13–14
Walk in the way of the good, and keep to the paths of the just. For the upright will abide in the land, and the innocent will remain in it.
Proverbs 2:20–21 (NRSV)

Several weeks ago, my wife and I were travelling on a fast road. We noticed what appeared to be a ribbon of rubbish blowing across the lane just ahead of us. But as we came closer, we saw that it was not rubbish but a duck with ducklings waddling behind across the road. I swerved past them, painfully aware that ours was the first in a line of cars coming their way. After my racing heart slowed down, I said, 'Is that duck crazy? Crossing a busy road?'

As soon as the words left my mouth, memories of some of my past choices flashed before me. Like a duck walking across a road, I have set out across moral boundaries. I engaged in promiscuous behaviour that resulted in depression, fear, guilt and shame.

In my distress, I asked God to show me a better way. And God did—leading me off the road of self-destructive thinking and living toward freedom in Christ. As I prayed and read God's word, my heart opened to walking a spiritual path that quieted my restless soul. The more we prayerfully seek God's will, the less we are inclined to wander into dangerous behaviour.

Prayer: *Dear God of freedom and right, thank you for leading us out of trouble when we place our trust in you. Amen*

Thought for the day: God can lead us from death and destruction to life and hope.

Michael Lewis (Virginia)

PRAYER FOCUS: THOSE WHO ARE SELF-DESTRUCTIVE

Faith Heroes

Read Romans 10:10–17
You, friends, must not become tired of doing good.
2 Thessalonians 3:13 (GNB)

'Dear Pastor, I recently found a Bible given to me in 1959 by Mr Steckman, a Sunday school teacher at your church. At that time I was 13, and a neighbour brought me to church. I am now a Christian and would like to thank Mr Steckman. If you have any information on how I could contact him, I would really appreciate it. In Christ, M.' My husband received this note in 2009—50 years after Mr Steckman handed the Bible to that young girl. Like the many faith heroes mentioned in Hebrews 11, Mr Steckman left this world without seeing the fruit of this gift of love.

Sometimes each of us may wonder, 'Am I having any effect? Am I drawing people to Jesus Christ?' The words of 2 Thessalonians 3:13 encourage us to persevere in doing good. Like Mr Steckman, we may never know that we made a difference in another person's life. M's note, however, confirms that our efforts are not in vain.

We may or may not see results in our lifetime, and our contributions may seem insignificant at the time we make them. But together with the labour of others, we can be certain our efforts will accomplish much. God will bring our work to fruition—if it takes 50 years or even longer.

Prayer: *Dear Lord, please use our efforts to share your saving grace, even beyond the days allotted to us. Amen*

Thought for the day: Whether or not we get to see it, every act of love bears fruit.

Link2Life: *Thank the people who are responsible for providing Bibles to those who do not have them.*

Pam Williams (Pennsylvania)

Lord of the Dance

Read Isaiah 55:1–5

Those who wait for the Lord shall renew their strength, they shall mount up with wings like eagles, they shall run and not be weary, they shall walk and not faint.

Isaiah 40:31 (NRSV)

My daughter was born with curved femur bones in her legs. As a child, she had difficulty running and walking. Discouraged by not being selected in sports and dance activities for much of her life, she always tried to accept her disappointment with a smile. As she grew up, she gained strength in her legs and began to participate in dance classes. I noticed that she had rhythm but lacked grace; she danced like a stick!

My daughter came home excited about a dancing show to be held at school. She loves dancing and music, and she had to perform well to be selected for the show. But all my efforts to help her failed. Then I sat with her and we read together in the Bible about water—specifically Isaiah 55:1: 'Come, all you who are thirsty, come to the waters' (NIV). I showed her some water and told her to be like that water, letting her body and mind flow without restriction and fear of rejection. She performed extremely well and was selected for the show. She had learned a lesson—not only about dancing but also for life. As we allow God's grace to work through us, God will help us walk—even dance—through the difficult steps of life!

Prayer: *Our wise and loving heavenly Father, thank you for teaching us. Help us to learn well what you teach us through your wonderful creation. Amen*

Thought for the day: God invites us to live without fear.

Beena Abraham (Karnataka, India)

PRAYER FOCUS: CHILDREN WITH DISABILITIES

Stop, Look, and Listen

Read Jeremiah 6:13–19

Stand at the crossroads and look; ask for the ancient paths, ask where the good way is, and walk in it, and you will find rest for your souls.
Jeremiah 6:16 (NIV)

As a child, I was taught to stop, look and listen before crossing the street. Through the prophet Jeremiah, God gave similar wise advice to the people of Judah 2700 years ago. The situation looked grim for the Southern Kingdom. Israel had fallen; enemies gathered on all sides and Judah rebelled. Jeremiah had the unpleasant task of delivering a message of doom, but in the midst of the message, Jeremiah dropped a gem of wisdom and hope in the scripture verse above: stop, look for 'the good way' and listen to (heed) the direction.

This principle applies in other situations as well. We all want personal peace and contentment, 'rest for our souls'. But how do we get this? When we stand at the crossroads of a difficult decision, rushing ahead blindly is unwise or worse. Instead, we can stop, look and ask, 'What does God want me to see in this situation?' We can ask for counsel from godly men and women, from God through prayer, and from scripture's ancient paths. Finally, after discerning the direction God has revealed at the crossroads, we can move forward. We can walk with confidence and peace down the 'good way' and find what we truly desire—rest for our souls.

Prayer: *Dear God, help us to discern your will when facing difficult decisions. Amen*

Thought for the day: Asking for guidance and heeding it is a mark of wisdom.

Link2Life: *Practise asking: 'What does God want me to see in this?'*

Michael Saum (Central Province, Kenya)

Someone's at the Door

Read 1 Timothy 6:17–19

Let mutual love continue. Do not neglect to show hospitality to strangers, for by doing that some have entertained angels without knowing it.
Hebrews 13:1–2 (NRSV)

It is easy for me to get trapped in the daily routine of life. I work, get paid, pay bills, go shopping. But am I doing enough of the most important things? Am I making a difference in God's world and for God's people by giving to others from a heart of love? As time passes, we may come to ignore those knocking at our door or begging at street corners. All they may want is something to eat or a warm coat to wear. How often do we tend to think, 'I give enough' or 'I give to my church and other charities' or 'My family comes first'?

One day a man who had knocked on my door many times arrived again. This time I asked him to leave without even listening to him. After a few minutes my son said, 'Dad, are we being Christian by turning him away?' His question was like a nudge from God. We got in the car and found the man walking down the road. We picked him up and took him home, showing hospitality as the scripture tells us to. My son gave some of his own money to help the man's needs.

Do we really give enough—time, money, assistance—in church and community? Even more, do we give without expecting something in return? After all, we are doing it for God and God's people.

Prayer: *Dear Lord, thank you for what we have. Keep us ever aware of those who have needs we can meet. Amen*

Thought for the day: Give freely, without expecting anything back.

Link2Life: *Think ahead of what you will say and how you will act toward the next person who asks you for help.*

Shaun McHardy (Western Cape, South Africa)

PRAYER FOCUS: FOR A RENEWED SENSE OF HEARTFELT GIVING

What Does This Have to Do with Jesus?

Read Colossians 3:12–17

Whatever you do, in word or deed, do everything in the name of the Lord Jesus, giving thanks to God the Father through him.
Colossians 3:17 (NRSV)

In our church during Sunday morning worship, the children come to the front for a special children's message. One Sunday, the speaker was using a maze with a ball-bearing rolling through it as a visual aid for his lesson. Five-year-old Hannah had listened patiently but finally asked, 'Just what has this got to do with Jesus?' At the time, our response was gentle laughter. But since then, this question has become an important part of our church community. It is a reminder to every church leader or committee that may at times lose sight of our true objective. It is also a personal question for every Christian.

When we lose our focus, the simple question—'What does this have to do with Jesus?'—can help us to remember our reason for what we are doing. This question can guide everything we do and say. When we become distracted by earthly concerns, we can remind ourselves about Christ and focus on him. This puts everything in perspective and can give us peace.

Prayer: *Dear Father, may we learn to look at every task as a part of your kingdom. Open our eyes and hearts to your will. Amen*

Thought for the day: What does the way you spend your time have to do with Jesus?

Harriet Outlaw (Alabama)

A Rough Ride

Read Luke 18:18–30

Jesus said to them all, 'If any want to become my followers, let them deny themselves and take up their cross daily and follow me.'
Luke 9:23 (NRSV)

It was going to be my first long bus ride. The person who sold me my ticket attempted to allay my fears by telling me that it was a nice journey over a smooth road. After talking with her for quite some time, I felt reassured and boarded the bus. Within a short time, I realised that what she had told me was not so. The drive was rough and full of jerks, at times even throwing me off my seat. I was not prepared for it, and I blamed her for not telling me the truth.

In today's Bible reading, the young ruler wanted to inherit eternal life. When Jesus told him to sell all that he had before following him, the young man chose not to follow. Jesus could have made the way appear easier for the young man, but instead he gave a true picture of the cost of discipleship.

Remembering my rough ride and the story in Luke 18, I thought of my journey in the Christian faith. When I was learning about Christ, I was told what it meant to follow him—that I would suffer hardships and difficulties and even rejection by my own family members. Because of this, when I chose to receive Christ, I was prepared to face the consequences. I knew what to expect, and when difficulty came I was not taken by surprise. This made my Christian journey easier.

Prayer: *Dear Lord, help us honestly to teach others what devotion to Christ really means. Amen*

Thought for the day: True discipleship asks us to walk a difficult road.

Pramila Barkataki (Maharashtra, India)

A New Future

Read Philippians 3:10–16

Forgetting what lies behind and straining forward to what lies ahead, I press on toward the goal for the prize of the heavenly call of God in Christ Jesus.

Philippians 3:13–14 (NRSV)

I often reminisce about events in my past. Some of them easily come to mind. But when I think about the future, I can only speculate.

The apostle Paul also considered both past and future. But what he wrote about forgetting the past (Philippians 3:13), I do not see as scrubbing the past from memory but as not allowing it to get in the way of our 'pressing on' (v. 14). My past is not free of sin, but because I confess Jesus Christ as Lord and Saviour, I have been forgiven that. The redemption that he brought by his life, death and resurrection, was for everyone—including me—and for all time.

Holding on to memories of a troubled or sinful past does not benefit our present or our future. Thankfully, our past can be transformed by Jesus Christ into light for the present and hope for the future. This memory of my past causes me to cherish even more the reality that Jesus Christ has redeemed my present and my future.

Prayer: *Gracious Lord Jesus, although we cannot see the future, we know that you will be there with us. That is more than enough. Amen*

Thought for the day: We can be set free from our past when we place our future in God's hands.

John Eyberg (Oklahoma)

In Christ's Name

Read Matthew 25:31–46

Jesus said, 'Truly I tell you, whoever gives you a cup of water to drink because you bear the name of Christ will by no means lose the reward.'
Mark 9:41 (NRSV)

I was seriously ill with bronchitis and unable to leave the house to shop for food. My Christian friends came to my aid. I knew that they were praying for my return to health, but their caring did not stop there.

One friend took my shopping list and went to the supermarket for me. This meant I was able to eat foods that would strengthen me. Another friend came and sat with me for a short while each day. This meant I was not lonely. She also kept me up to date with all the church news. This meant I could pray specifically. I had time to pray even more than I usually do. One person took me to the doctor so I could obtain the correct medicine. Yet another friend posted my letters for me.

My helpers were all busy people themselves, but they made time to help me in the name of Christ. They were doing what Christ instructs us to do.

Now that I have returned to full health, I too can visit the sick. I can help housebound people to feel less lonely, and I can aid those who need basic help. This is the way God wants us to live.

Prayer: *Thank you, faithful God, for those who help us in our need. May they receive your blessing as you have promised. Amen*

Thought for the day: Each of us can both give and receive.

Link2Life: *Offer to do an errand for someone in your church who is ill.*

Carol Purves (Cumbria, England)

From Generation to Generation

Read Deuteronomy 11:1–7, 18–21

It was your own eyes that saw all these great things the Lord has done.
Deuteronomy 11:7 (NIV)

How do you know what happened a hundred years ago? Two hundred years ago? You weren't there. How do we learn about what took place in history? The answer is that people who were there wrote about it. They told their children about it. They passed on their knowledge to family and friends. Important information is handed down from generation to generation. That's how history gets to us.

God did a wonderful work, leading the chosen people out of captivity. But there was more to come. God commanded the people who experienced deliverance to tell their children and their children's children what had happened. God didn't want the people to forget the covenant. God was keeping the promises made to them, and they needed to keep their promises, too.

We are the only ones with first-hand knowledge of what God has done in our lives. Small experiences and great ones form our history with God. As with the history we have received, the only way for our knowledge of God to reach others is for us to pass it on. That's our privilege and our obligation.

Prayer: *Dear God, help us to tell others what you have done for us. As Jesus taught us, we pray, 'Father, hallowed be your name, your kingdom come. Give us each day our daily bread. Forgive us our sins, for we also forgive everyone who sins against us. And lead us not into temptation.'**

Thought for the day: What events can I list in my history of God's acts?

Link2Life: *Prepare a list of your history of God's actions.*

Richard Mabry (Texas)

* Luke 11:2–4 (NIV)

A Time for Everything

Read Ecclesiastes 3:1–8

For everything there is a season, and a time for every matter under heaven: a time to be born, and a time to die; a time to plant, and a time to pluck up what is planted.

Ecclesiastes 3:1–2 (NRSV)

The first time I read *Mesto Vstrechi* (the Russian edition of *The Upper Room*), which means 'Meeting Place', was in the winter of 2008. I stayed up all night reading the meditations. I wanted to be fed immediately by spiritual grace and discover how people live in God on different sides of the globe. When I read the testimony of a woman who had been reading *The Upper Room* for 70 years, I was upset. I asked, 'Lord, why have you given me this resource only now, when many people have been reading it all their lives?'

Then I remembered receiving my Bible 17 years ago; a friend gave it to me as a present from abroad. I realised from reading my Bible that God loves me. Moreover, God has given me a church where I can go and receive such grace as these meditations, written by my brothers and sisters in Christ, about what it means to live in faith daily. God consoles me through these words: 'For everything there is a season and a time for every matter under heaven.' I continue to read *Mesto Vstrechi*, and I'm grateful now for this resource that helps me live my faith more fully.

Prayer: *O God, thank you for our relationship with you and for reassurance that this happens at the right time. Amen*

Thought for the day: Our faith connects us with God's people everywhere.

Galina Samson (Voronezh, Russia)

Numbering our Days

Read Psalm 63:1–8

Teach us to number our days aright that we may gain a heart of wisdom.

Psalm 90:12 (NIV)

This visit from my family was to be unforgettable. About ten minutes into the visit, Dad found an excuse for him and me to go to the shop. While Dad was telling me that something was wrong with Mum, my mother was telling my wife how Dad had put a secret code on the telephone that prevented her from using it. Not long after this, Mum was diagnosed with Alzheimer's. She died a few years later in a nursing home.

Her death caused me to reflect on how fragile life is. But of course I am not the first to do so. The psalmist, knowing this, prayed centuries ago, 'Teach us to number our days' (NIV). Most of us ignore the fact that our days are limited. The sun rises, we awake, we go to work, we entertain ourselves. The sun sets, we sleep, we awake to start the cycle again. That's life. But some tomorrow we will not wake up.

Though we may number our days with birthday parties and New Year's Eve festivities, we can also number them by measuring our closeness to God. I am determined to apply myself to knowing God more intimately. I will read the scripture as more than a duty. I will praise God in song and be unashamed. I will seek a 'heart of wisdom' (Psalm 90:12, NIV).

Prayer: *Dear Lord, remind us that our time here is limited and that knowing and pleasing you should be the work of our life. Amen*

Thought for the day: How do I measure the quality of my life?

Thomas Buice (Florida)

Forgiveness of All Sins

Read Acts 26:9–18

Jesus said, 'Drink from [the cup], all of you. This is my blood of the covenant, which is poured out for many for the forgiveness of sins.'
Matthew 26:27–28 (NIV)

As a child, I often spent Saturday nights at a friend's house nearby and then went to church with them. One Sunday while kneeling at the altar to take Communion, I noticed that the offertory plate had been placed on the floor in front of the altar. Several notes of money were lying close to where I knelt. After eyeing them for several seconds, I reached out to take them. I was immediately thwarted in this effort by the mother of my friend.

I realise now that it was a childish impulse and not a fatal sin, but back then I felt extremely guilty for my actions. I was relieved when the neighbours did not mention it again and particularly that they didn't tell my mother.

For many years that was my main memory about Communion. But as an adult I began to study the meaning of the Last Supper. The message of Jesus' dying so that I might be forgiven became a powerful foundation of my belief. For the first time, and finally, I felt forgiven for my sins, no matter how big I believed them to be.

Now I have the privilege of serving Communion at the same altar that so many years ago was the scene of my youthful offence, welcoming each one as among the forgiven—as am I.

Prayer: *Dear heavenly Father, thank you for sending us your Son to show us how much you love us. Help us to feel the forgiveness he brought, that we can draw closer to you. Amen*

Thought for the day: Feeling forgiven allows us to love ourselves and everyone we meet.

John Dean (New Mexico)

God's Constant Presence

Read Psalm 121

The Lord watches over you—the Lord is your shade at your right hand.
Psalm 121:5 (NIV)

Outside on a sunny day, shadows are our constant companions. When we move along, they move along with us—connected to us. Regardless of our pace, our shadow keeps up; it is impossible to separate ourselves from it.

This is what I think of when I read that the Lord is the 'shade at [our] right hand'. I see God attached to us as determinedly as our shadow. Sometimes our shadow is lengthened and more obvious; other times it is shortened and not so easily seen. God's presence is the same. At times we can clearly see God moving in our lives. At other times God's work isn't as obvious, and we may doubt that God is even there. During these latter times, we can depend on the word of God, that is always true, and know that God is forever with us.

When we see the shadows cast by our bodies and how they cannot be disengaged from us, may we be reminded that it is the same with the Lord. God is always with us.

Prayer: *Dear God our Companion, thank you for your constant presence. Amen*

Thought for the day: God is more constant and connected to us than our shadow is.

Pat Rowland (Tennessee)

PRAYER FOCUS: THOSE WHO ARE ALONE AND FRIGHTENED

Our Way, or God's?

Read Matthew 11:28–30

Jesus said, 'My yoke is easy, and my burden is light.'
Matthew 11:30 (NRSV)

I was resting on the settee in the living-room when I noticed my four-year-old son in the hall. He was crying as he struggled to open a container with a tight lid. I asked him to bring the container to me so I could help him, but he resolutely wanted to open it himself. He continued to cry, and his frustration grew. When exhaustion overcame him, he finally decided to allow me to help. He then saw how easy it was for me. He could have avoided the frustration and trauma had he come to me earlier.

This incident became a spiritual lesson for me about how to handle difficult situations. Too often, rather than seeking God's help, we try our own methods to solve our problems—and we often end up frustrated or in tears. But God's promise is before us: 'Come to me, all you that are weary and are carrying heavy burdens, and I will give you rest.' God has the solution to our problems: believe in and trust in God's word—and ask for God's help.

Prayer: *Dear loving God, help us understand that with you all things are possible. We know that we can place our problems in your care and that in you we can find rest. Amen*

Thought for the day: Go to God first.

Yaneth Orozco Z. (Valle del Cauca, Colombia)

PRAYER FOCUS: PARENTS OF YOUNG CHILDREN

From Despair to Joy

Read Lamentations 3:55–57

We know that in all things God works for the good of those who love him, who have been called according to his purpose.
Romans 8:28 (NIV)

Depression is a debilitating illness. I know from first-hand experience the effect it can have on a person's life. For more than ten years, I have lived with this devastating disease that afflicts millions of people each year. Before I could place a name on the sadness that often lasted for weeks at a time, I felt hopeless. I found it difficult to concentrate and experienced decreased interest in activities that I had previously enjoyed.

Not knowing what to do, I cried out to God for help. I made a commitment to pray and to read God's word each day. As I acknowledged my fears, I felt God's hand rescuing me from despair. Although my road to recovery has taken years of working with skilled physicians and counsellors, I always believed that if I prayed and trusted, God would turn my sorrow into joy (see Jeremiah 31:13).

Lamentations 3 is a reminder that prayer is a strong source of power available to us. When peace seems remote, God promises us to be near and to turn our struggles into something good.

Prayer: *Dear heavenly Father, thank you for the privilege of prayer. As we walk through this day, remind us of the transformation that you can bring to our lives when we call upon you. Amen*

Thought for the day: Prayer opens the door for God's power and strength to fill us.

James C. Hendrix (Indiana)

Safe Places

Read Exodus 17:1–7
I am the Lord your God, who brought you up out of Egypt. Open wide your mouth and I will fill it.
Psalm 81:10 (NIV)

Since we moved to a new area, our cat Sara has stayed indoors. Her new outdoor surroundings, although intriguing, terrify her. Often she paces in front of the door to the garden, miaowing longingly to go out. However, when I open the door, encouraging her to explore her new stretch of grass and trees, she panics and runs for safety. I'm always sad when she passes up potential pleasure out of fear.

Although my adjustment to the move was less difficult than Sara's, in less obvious parts of my life I too shrink back from new opportunities out of a similar fear. Sometimes those opportunities entail entering a new ministry, making a job change or forging a new friendship. In these situations, God seems to be opening wide the door that leads toward fresh, new settings. Sadly, too often my initial response is like Sara's—I run for safety, toward the familiar.

When the Israelites left Egypt, they too struggled with facing the unknown. When they thirsted in the wilderness, turning back toward familiar Egypt seemed easier and safer than trusting God to provide. Like the Israelites, I am guilty of looking back to the familiar when God offers me new opportunities. Yet I am encouraged not to cower but to walk confidently into the wide-open spaces God provides. I can step forward, knowing that God is already there.

Prayer: *Dear Lord, thank you for your presence. Help us daily to trust you to provide for us. Give us courage to walk where you lead. Amen*

Thought for the day: We can trust in God's presence and provision every day.

Olive Lois Fisher (Kentucky)

Welcome!

Read John 14:1–6

No eye has seen, no ear has heard, no mind has conceived what God has prepared for those who love him.

1 Corinthians 2:9 (NIV)

On a recent overseas trip, my wife and I arrived at our destination at 5:30AM after a 20-hour flight. We had expected a delay in being transferred to our hotel and were delighted to be greeted at the airport by a driver sent for us. Our joy increased when, on arriving at the hotel at 7AM, we were welcomed and told, 'Your room is ready.' We were grateful that everything had been prepared for us.

This made me think how much more wonderful it is to know that when we make the great journey from this life to the next through the doorway of death, we will be met not by a driver but by a wonderful friend waiting to greet us and tell us, 'Your room is ready.'

Our friend and Saviour has promised, 'In my Father's house are many rooms… I am going there to prepare a place for you… I will come back and take you to be with me that you also may be where I am' (John 14:2–3, NIV). This is Christ's promise to all who put their faith in him. What a wonderful and thrilling prospect!

Prayer: *Thank you, gracious God, for all your promises to us and for your faithfulness in keeping them. Today and every day we trust in you. Amen*

Thought for the day: At the end of life's journey, we will be greeted by our loving Saviour.

Bill Willis (New South Wales, Australia)

Sowing and Reaping

Read Psalm 126

Let us not grow weary in doing what is right, for we will reap at harvest time, if we do not give up.
Galatians 6:9 (NRSV)

Three years ago my family purchased an acre of land. Sadly, the land was devoid of trees and plants. Soon, my husband and I took on the task of planting trees, shrubs and fruit-bearing plants.

The task turned out to be harder and more expensive than we thought. Many of the plants simply did not thrive and had to be replaced. Weeds, insects and plant diseases are insidious. We had to use herbicides and insecticides and fertilise and water continually. Even so, though the work was exhausting, we now notice the differences. The grass looks lovely when we mow it; the first trees we planted are beginning to spread their branches to provide shade; the lilies and amaryllis are a joy; and my son loves to pick the fresh strawberries.

Doing God's work is similar. Sometimes the work seems overwhelming compared to the results we see. However, the Bible encourages us to continue (see Galatians 6:9 and 1 Corinthians 15:58). Today's scripture selection is a source of comfort and encouragement to me in doing God's work. We may not see immediate results, but God is merciful, and in due time we will reap with joy.

Prayer: *Creator God, help us work with faith, confident in the knowledge that what you sow through us will bear fruit. Amen*

Thought for the day: When we work for God our efforts are never in vain.

Pérsida Ramos (North Carolina)

For All of Us

Read Colossians 1:15–23

Jesus said to [Martha], 'I am the resurrection and the life. Those who believe in me, even though they die, will live, and everyone who lives and believes in me will never die.'
John 11:25–26 (NRSV)

We often use a mirrored cross on the altar of our church. Its front is smooth and plain, but the sides and the top are a mosaic. Broken pieces of mirror are glued on the cross, with large and small spaces between them.

In a recent worship service, I was directly in front of this cross. All I could see was my reflection in it. I sat there for a few minutes thinking, 'This cross is for me. Jesus died on a cross because of me. He gave his life for me.'

Although deeply touched, I also felt guilt and shame and finally became so uncomfortable that I decided to change seats with someone else. Later, looking again at the cross, I could no longer see only myself. I saw the faces of my friends, my loved ones—my church family. Some images appeared broken, some cracked; some small, others very large. Reflecting on this, I realised that the cross belongs to all of us. Jesus died for all of us. None of us is worthy; we all are sinners. But in Jesus' sacrifice, God's grace is given freely to all of us so that we may live in the light of this grace for ever.

Prayer: *Dear heavenly Father, your grace and love have saved us and set us free. For this we love you and praise you for ever. In Jesus' name. Amen*

Thought for the day: Jesus died for you and you and you—and me.

Freda Crumpton (Alabama)

Uncertain Times

Read Luke 12:22–31

Jesus answered, 'What is humanly impossible is possible for God.'
Luke 18:27 (GNB)

We live in uncertain times. Both the news and our personal situations may fill us with anxiety. Recently while I was recovering from back surgery and the complications of an infection, my company made me redundant. I wondered, 'How is my family going to survive until I get a new job? What will happen to our plans for the future?'

My mother and many friends reminded me that I was on their prayer circle's list of concerns and that God hears the prayers of the righteous, those who want to be close to God and try to live their life accordingly. People I did not even know were praying for me.

I began to see that God's blessings were flowing to me through many people, some I never would have imagined. A friend reminded me that God created all things good. God continues to create, and all things will be good again. Each time uncertainty creeps in, I remind myself that God is all-loving, all-powerful, and all-knowing. God is ever present at the potter's wheel, using our good times and bad to mould us into the people God wants us to be.

Prayer: *In you, O God of hope and joy, all things came into being, including each of us. Help us to be mindful of your presence and to walk with you in hope and faith, seeking your will, not our own. Amen*

Thought for the day: God leads us into the future one step at a time.

Mark H. Anderson (Pennsylvania)

Borrowed Equipment

Read 1 Samuel 17:32–40, 50

Let us throw off everything that hinders... and let us run with perseverance the race marked out for us.
Hebrews 12:1 (NIV)

I've always loved the Bible's story of David the shepherd boy who defeats Goliath with a sling and a stone. Recently, I realised that David had to take something off in order to succeed in this mission. King Saul tried to protect David by giving him Saul's armour. David quickly discovered that Saul's heavy equipment hindered him. He removed the king's armour and approached Goliath unhindered, armed only with his usual shepherd's supplies and his strong trust in God.

Meditating on this story, I wonder how often I try to serve God wearing someone else's 'equipment'. Of course, we all can learn from the good example of others. But when asked to teach Sunday school, do I think I must imitate the previous teacher? Do I study a method of evangelism and then mimic its exact words when I share my faith? Do I weigh myself down copying someone else's style? Am I afraid to serve God just as I am?

I have decided that it's time to drop the weight of trying to be like others and to be myself instead. The Lord has given each of us unique gifts. We don't need borrowed equipment. We can all learn from David, taking off whatever hinders us and trusting God for help in using our God-given abilities.

Prayer: *Thank you, mighty Lord, for equipping each of us uniquely. Give us courage to be ourselves as we serve you. Amen*

Thought for the day: What hinders me from serving God freely?

Marion Speicher Brown (Florida)

A Touch of Jesus

Read Matthew 9:18–26

A woman… came up behind [Jesus] and touched the edge of his cloak. She said to herself, 'If I only touch his cloak, I will be healed.'
Matthew 9:20–21 (NIV)

Part of my five years on a US naval ship included three six-month deployments. Each time that I was away, I ached to be with my family, longing for the day we would be reunited. Every few weeks, post would be brought on board with letters and pictures from my wife. Sometimes we would pull into a port where I could telephone her. These little touches with my wife made a connection that turned my sorrow to joy.

I see a connection between my attitude at sea and our attitudes about the Christian life. We yearn for a connection with Christ, but in the meantime, we may feel alone or even abandoned. But we are not alone. Christ has left us many ways to touch him. Like my wife, Christ gives us love letters in the Bible and pictures in creation. Christ gives us friendship with God's other children, and he always has a line open so that we can talk to him in prayer. We do not have to wait to get to heaven to touch Christ's garment and be made whole. We can do it now.

Prayer: *Dearest Lord Jesus, help us to connect with you each day, to touch you in any way that we can as we pray, 'Our Father which art in heaven, Hallowed be thy name. Thy kingdom come. Thy will be done, as in heaven, so in earth. Give us day by day our daily bread. And forgive us our sins; for we also forgive every one that is indebted to us. And lead us not into temptation; but deliver us from evil.'* Amen*

Thought for the day: If we seek Christ, we will find him.

Jeff Boyer (Washington)

Teaching by Example

Read 1 Timothy 4:6–16

Do not let anyone look down on you because you are young, but be an example for the believers in your speech, your conduct, your love, faith and purity.

1 Timothy 4:12 (GNB)

I have learned many lessons from my six-year-old daughter. One day, I asked her to turn off the electric fan. She turned it off using her foot. In Thai culture, feet are considered the lowest part of the body and one never points or uses the feet to touch anything.

'Why did you use your foot?' I asked.

She responded, 'I saw you do it that way.'

Her response made me more aware of my actions. Parents' behaviour influences young children. From their daily experiences within the family, children learn and reflect the actions of their parents. Sometimes we believe our actions are too insignificant to be noticed by others, but this is not the case.

The same is true of our Christian faith and practice. God wants us to be the light of the world. We are to be examples to those around us as we express 'love, faith and purity' in our everyday speech and behaviour.

Prayer: *Dear heavenly Lord, wherever we are and whatever we do, let us be an example of the love of Jesus Christ. Amen*

Thought for the day: Can other people see Christ in my actions?

Adisorn Mathusawan (Chiang Rai Province, Thailand)

Blessing in Obeying

Read Matthew 4:18–22
As the Holy Spirit says, 'Today, if you hear his voice, do not harden your hearts as in the rebellion, as on the day of testing in the wilderness.'
Hebrews 3:7–8 (NRSV)

While I was a student I heard the Lord's voice calling me to professional ministry, but I ran away from it. In time I was given two children and at that point, according to my own convenience, I decided everything was all right; I was not open to God's call. Eighteen years later I heard Christ say to me, 'Follow me, and I will make you fish for people' (Matthew 4:19). 'Such absurdity,' I thought. But the more I tried to ignore the leading, the more this verse resounded in my mind. I protested: I had a family; I had no savings; I'm not an eloquent speaker. But the words of scripture kept resonating in my mind. When I finally surrendered, I said, 'If you can use me, I entrust myself to you.' I experienced indescribable peace.

Now, over the age of 40, I have left behind my secular position. The three years of training at seminary were difficult, but I received abundant blessings. In a miraculous way, my needs were met. More than anything, I learned to trust God completely. It was a late start, but those years of secular work were necessary; they taught me much that I now use in my ministry. Nothing is wasted in God's work.

We can listen to and obey the Lord's voice without fear. When we trust in the Lord and take the first step, we will see God's great work!

Prayer: *Dear Loving God, give us faith humbly to listen to and obey your voice. We pray in Jesus' name. Amen*

Thought for the day: Everything in our lives can be used to serve God.

Makoto Nose (Tokyo, Japan)

God's Grace-filled Love

Read Isaiah 43:1–3
The Lord told Paul, 'My grace is sufficient for you, for my power is made perfect in weakness.'
2 Corinthians 12:9 (NIV)

A blanket of fresh snow made the driveway so icy that I slipped to the ground, injuring my shoulder. Healing came slowly but never completely. Months passed. Prayers for my full recovery seemed to go unanswered. Then I recalled how the apostle Paul prayed to God to remove his painful affliction, his 'thorn in the flesh'. But God did not heal Paul. Rather, God told him, 'My grace is sufficient for you, for my power is made perfect in weakness.'

My shoulder still troubles me at times. But I find strength as I recall God's words to Paul. At every instance of pain, those words serve as a reminder that God is always with me. God's love gives me strength, even when I experience weakness in my shoulder.

We may suffer pain from physical affliction, loss of a loved one or a job, stress in a relationship. We can pray for relief and wait for the Lord to answer. But whenever we endure continuing challenge, we can find strength in knowing that God loves us and cares for us. With that assurance, we can say with Paul, 'When I am weak, then I am strong' (2 Corinthians 12:10, NIV). God's strength will carry us through our weakness.

Prayer: *Dear Lord, help us to feel your power within us in our times of struggle and pain. In Jesus' name. Amen*

Thought for the day: Even though we are not perfect, we can be strong.

Gerald W. Bauer (Ohio)

A Merciful Parent

Read Psalm 107:1, 23–32

Because of his great love for us, God, who is rich in mercy, made us alive with Christ even when we were dead in transgressions—it is by grace you have been saved.
Ephesians 2:4–5 (NIV)

I live with chronic depression, and I used to suffer from a guilty conscience. I thought God was always angry, counting my sins and eager to punish me, until one night God was revealed to me as a gentle father.

I was putting my children to bed after a long day. I kissed them and said goodnight. When I turned to go, I was overcome by how much I love them. Almost immediately, I felt God speak to my heart, 'Then why don't you believe that I love you, my daughter?'

I realised that God loves me unconditionally, as I love my children. When my children do something wrong, I do not stop loving them. I discipline them; I guide them back to the right path; and when they are sorry, I forgive them. God is a merciful parent, loving me even as I sin. Though upset by some of my actions, God guides me in love. When I repent, God rejoices and forgives me.

I still suffer from depression, but I know now that I have a Father who cares for me, walking with me through dark times and loving me in spite of myself.

Prayer: *Dear God, you are merciful and loving. Thank you. Help us to reflect your love to those around us so that they too may know your great kindness. Amen*

Thought for the day: God's love never fails.

Rachel Lerch (Ontario, Canada)

Stuck in the Mud

Read Psalm 40:1–13

'You hypocrite, first take the plank out of your own eye, and then you will see clearly to remove the speck from your brother's eye.'
Luke 6:42 (NIV)

As I walked in the fields with my friend's three children after an especially wet few weeks, the ground was very muddy. The older two children, sure-footed as cats, raced ahead while I walked with the youngest child. He is only three, and still struggles to negotiate the uneven hillocks and ditches that surround their home. At one particularly boggy place he found that he was unable to move, as both his boots stuck firmly in the mud. He needed help, but as I tried to go to his aid I found that my own boot was also trapped. I had to extricate myself before I could pull him out.

Sin seems to stick to us like mud, not only holding our feet but blurring our vision. The psalmist, overwhelmed by sin, writes that he cannot see clearly and calls out to the Lord for help (Psalm 40:12–13). Often it is our own weaknesses that irritate us when we see them in others; we take far longer to acknowledge the same weaknesses in ourselves. Jesus' message is very blunt—sort out your own mess first. I couldn't help my young friend until my own feet were free from the mud. In the same way we need to be rescued from our own pride and selfishness before holding out a hand to others.

Prayer: *Father, show us clearly the things that hold us back from growing more like Jesus. Please give us the humility to ask for help. Amen*

Thought for the day: One muddy boot can ruin a gleaming floor.

Carol Griffin, Shropshire, England

PRAYER FOCUS: TO SEE THE 'PLANK' IN MY OWN EYE

Spiritual Endurance

Read 1 Corinthians 9:24–27

Do you not know that in a race all the runners run, but only one gets the prize? Run in such a way as to get the prize. Everyone who competes in the games goes into strict training. They do it to get a crown that will not last; but we do it to get a crown that will last forever.

1 Corinthians 9:24–25 (NIV)

In order to run a marathon, I must discipline my mind and my body to prepare for the race. Each morning, I venture out before sunrise with my feet beating the pavement for five miles. Admittedly, some mornings I would rather stay in bed. However, I know that unless I prepare myself well, I will not be able to accept the challenge when race day comes.

My spiritual life—especially my life of prayer—is a matter of similar discipline. When I am willing to meet with God daily, I can 'run the race' faithfully, and ultimately I will claim my reward. Living daily as a Christian requires commitment, strength of character and dependence on the Spirit's help. At times, negativity and discouragement can overshadow the good that God brings every day. During those times, I can rely on God's word from Paul in 1 Corinthians to see me through day by day until I reach the finish.

Prayer: *Dear God, please take our hands in yours as we go through this day. Help us to trust that you will give us strength day by day to follow Christ. Amen*

Thought for the day: How do I prepare myself to run the race faithfully?

Terri Meehan (Surrey, England)

Daisy's Gift

Read Luke 21:1–4

Jesus said, 'Give, and it will be given to you. A good measure, pressed down, shaken together, running over, will be put into your lap; for the measure you give will be the measure you get back.'
Luke 6:38 (NRSV)

'This can't be right,' I thought as I uneasily scanned the scene. A rusty old caravan stood before me, surrounded by dilapidated cars, broken appliances, empty bottles and weeds. As a Communion steward for my church, I take Communion once a month to housebound members, and Daisy was new among those I visit. When I knocked on the door, a white-haired woman leaning heavily on a stick and wearing a ragged dressing-gown greeted me. 'Come in,' she smiled, and I walked into a modest room with threadbare furniture.

One later Sunday when I visited, Daisy told me about a marvellous gift she had just received. 'My niece gave me $50—can you imagine!' This was wealth indeed for Daisy.

'What will you buy?' I asked her.

'I was thinking about clothes,' she said. 'But I wrote a cheque for the church instead and told them to put it toward our outreach to the foster children's home. I can't do much, but I can do that.' I was stunned. As I drove home, I reassessed my recent decision to cut back on my church giving. Daisy taught me what giving really means.

Prayer: *Holy God, help us to give as you desire—a good measure, pressed down and running over. Amen*

Thought for the day: Even in scarcity, we can find ways to give.

Link2Life: *Visit a housebound member of your church.*

Linda Ross (California)

Spiritual Maturity

Read Matthew 25:14–30

When I was a child, I spoke like a child, I thought like a child, I reasoned like a child; when I became an adult, I put an end to childish ways.
1 Corinthians 13:11 (NRSV)

When my daughter was seven years old, I asked her to wash the dishes. She washed the dishes, tidied up and called me. When I walked into the kitchen, I praised her for doing her work so well. She said, 'Now I'm a housewife, aren't I?' We smiled and embraced. I saw that she liked being grown up, and I was proud of my daughter.

In a much more significant sense, the Lord is pleased to see how we become mature Christians and good managers of our spiritual gifts, abilities and resources. Our heavenly father rejoices when we grow up spiritually and use our gifts more fully. At first we learn how to do lots of things ourselves, providing for our own needs and the needs of our family and supporting our church. Then we give to other people, families and churches. When we grow in using our gifts and talents, we can bless the people around us, in the place where we live, and in the whole world.

Seeing children learn responsibility is a joy. So is watching adults mature in every sphere of their lives. And churches growing in 'bringing people to faith in Christ' are a special joy. When we grow, as we are meant to, the Lord looks at us from heaven and rejoices.

Prayer: *Thank you, God, for helping us to leave behind our childish ways and to mature as Christians. Help us to bring you joy. In the name of Jesus Christ. Amen*

Thought for the day: The Lord rejoices when we mature spiritually.

Eduard Khegay (Moscow, Russia)

God's 'No'

Read Isaiah 55:6–13

*'My thoughts are not your thoughts, neither are your ways my ways,'
declares the Lord.*

Isaiah 55:8 (NIV)

After six months of unemployment, my husband, David, had an interview for his 'dream' job. He was almost assured of getting it. Almost. Then he received a rejection letter. David was as dejected as I had ever seen him. How could this have happened? We had trusted God, and now all we could do was agonise over this rejection.

One month later, we read in the newspaper that the company had closed its offices. Had David got that job, he would have been unemployed again within 30 days. What we thought was terrible, God turned to good. Soon after, David got a job closer to home, one that he has been happy with for the last five years.

How many times do we assume that an apparent 'no' to our prayers is evidence that God doesn't care about us? Nothing could be further from the truth! In fact, the apostle Paul wrote, 'We know that in all things God works for the good of those who love him, who have been called according to his purpose' (Romans 8:28, NIV). What we think is good for us may not be good at all, and what appears to be awful at one time can open a door to something better. God knows us so completely that even an answer of 'no' can be for our good.

Prayer: *Dear God, teach us patience as we wait for you, trusting in your infinite wisdom. Amen*

Thought for the day: With God, a 'no' can be a step toward something even better.

Toni Wilbarger (Ohio)

Decisions, Decisions!

Read Matthew 18:21–35

Do not be overcome by evil, but overcome evil with good.
Romans 12:21 (NRSV)

My friend César had a decision to make: should he help someone who had hurt and maligned him? He decided to put aside what had happened between them in the past. With humility and Christian love, he looked beyond the animosity and showed the other person the love that the Holy Spirit had poured out into his heart. Love triumphed over resentment.

In scripture we find people facing similar decisions. King David had the opportunity to destroy Saul, but instead he said, 'The Lord forbid that I should do this thing to my lord, the Lord's anointed' (1 Samuel 24:6, NRSV). Jonathan decided to defy his father by staying on the side of justice and defending David.

Often we too are confronted with challenges and important decisions. Some have a lasting impact. Each day we can consciously decide whether to serve God or ourselves. Choosing to serve God will fill our hearts with joy.

Prayer: *Dear God, may we desire to do your will. We pray as Jesus taught us, saying, 'Our Father which art in heaven, Hallowed be thy name. Thy kingdom come. Thy will be done in earth, as it is in heaven. Give us this day our daily bread. And forgive us our debts, as we forgive our debtors. And lead us not into temptation, but deliver us from evil: For thine is the kingdom, and the power, and the glory, for ever. Amen'**

Thought for the day: Every decision offers a chance to serve God.

Link2Life: *Each time you face a choice in the next 24 hours, pause for a few seconds to consider how your decision can serve God's purposes.*

Andria D. Amore Chinea (Tennessee)

Who is my Neighbour?

Read Luke 10:25–37
You shall love your neighbour as yourself.
Matthew 22:39 (NRSV)

Each Sunday in worship, our pastor invites the children to come forward for a special time together. He asked them what they needed to live. 'Food,' came one response. 'Water' and 'house' were volunteered. Then a young girl said firmly, 'A neighbour.' Murmurs of agreement echoed in the sanctuary, and my eyes filled with tears.

My heart wandered to the faces of several neighbours in my life. An elderly neighbour always had time for my two sons when they knocked on her door for a visit. She shared her love of flowers, and the recipes passed down from her grandmother became our family's favourites. When we moved to a new area, a new neighbour brought a plate of sandwiches on moving day to welcome us to the neighbourhood. Her calm spirit became a source of strength for my family. Other neighbours' quiet acts of kindness came to mind. In their friendship and grace, I saw Christlike action.

My thoughts turned to Jesus' words about loving our neighbours. Remembering special friends was comforting, but questions arose. What kind of neighbour am I? Am I showing Jesus' love to those along my path, as others have loved me?

Prayer: *Thank you, Lord, for helping us to become more loving neighbours. Amen*

Thought for the day: God can speak through acts of kindness.

Anne Cole Aker (Virginia)

Enough?

Read 1 Timothy 6:6–12

Better a little with the fear of the Lord than great wealth with turmoil.
Proverbs 15:16 (NIV)

I recently read in the newspaper about how my country has been affected by the global economic crisis. The article mentioned my country's average income per person. When I compared my salary to that, I found that I earn less than the average.

Sadness crossed my heart. 'I suppose my wife and I are poor,' I thought. 'Though we are in the same boat as 100 million other people in my country, another 100 million people have a more affluent and peaceful life.'

But is it true that they have a peaceful life? Do the 100 million people whose income is above mine have a peaceful life? Reading 1 Timothy 6:6–12 I am reminded of contentment, which means that I enjoy all God's grace given to me without comparing myself to others. I also remember that, according to Proverbs 15:16, 'Better a little with the fear of the LORD than great wealth with turmoil' (NIV). So far, my wife, my two-year-old son, and I have a meal every day; we have never had to beg for bread. We have what we need. And we know that God will never leave us alone.

I ask the Almighty to forgive my worrying about my household's future. I want to remember that God's hand is upon my life.

Prayer: *Dear God, we ask for your mercy. Help us to let go of our worries and trust you to provide. Amen*

Thought for the day: God never leaves us alone.

Bayu Probo (Jakarta, Indonesia)

Half-Way Obedience

Read Luke 3:7–17
John the Baptist said, 'Whoever has two shirts must give one to the man who has none, and whoever has food must share it.'
Luke 3:11 (GNB)

One winter night, Joe, one of my son David's friends, called to take David to a concert. I greeted Joe and asked, 'How are you?' Blowing on his hands, he said, 'It's terribly cold tonight; my hands are freezing!' 'Wait just a minute,' I said. Going into my bedroom, I got out an extra pair of gloves and took them to Joe. With a smile, I said, 'Scripture says, "If you have an extra pair of gloves, lend them to someone who has none." Keep these until warm weather.'

After they had gone, I became troubled about what I had said. John the Baptist didn't say 'lend', he said 'give'. I looked up the passage in Luke and realised I had gone only halfway toward obeying the teaching. Especially in a time of high unemployment and repossessions of families' homes, God calls us to radical generosity. I'm glad that many churches, including my own, organise food donations for the poor; some provide clothing either free or at a low price, and some strive to provide housing for the homeless.

The next time I saw Joe, I said, 'The gloves are yours to keep. I had misquoted the Bible; it tells us to give, not merely to lend.' I did that because I believe that living by God's word is the way to life.

Prayer: *Living God, help us to hear in our hearts the full meaning of your word, and give us grace to live by it, each minute of our lives.*

Thought for the day: God wants us to give with open hands.

Link2Life: *Contact your nearest homeless shelter, and provide some warm clothes for those who need them.*

Fred Cloud (Tennessee)

Bidden or Not Bidden

Read Jeremiah 29:4–7

Seek the peace… of the city to which I [the Lord] have carried you… Pray to the Lord for it, because if it prospers, you too will prosper.
Jeremiah 29:7 (NIV)

Several years ago my husband and I moved from a bustling city to a quiet town to run an inn. We went from total retirement to busy days of welcoming guests, cooking and cleaning. But we loved meeting the people and sensed that God had led us to this as a ministry.

Still, I occasionally wondered about our purpose here. Then I found the words from Jeremiah that we read today. So we laid paths and planted a flower garden for both guests and residents to enjoy. We also began to pray for our neighbours. Their concerns are a microcosm of those found anywhere—broken relationships, illness, job loss, deaths. The celebrations are also familiar—weddings, restored health, rewarding employment, births. After three years we felt very much at home in this little spot to which God had carried us.

Then my husband was stricken with a terminal illness and in two months was gone. I sometimes cry out to God, 'Why did you bring us here, then leave me alone, without Roy?' But Isaiah 54:5 answers, 'Your Maker is your husband—the Lord Almighty' (NIV). And Psalm 46:1 promises, 'God is our refuge and strength, an ever-present help in trouble' (NIV). In my husband Roy's memory I have placed in the garden a plaque that reads, 'Bidden or not bidden, God is present.' I meet God in our garden and continue to pray for my neighbours.

Prayer: *O God, thank you for being with us wherever we dwell. Hold close those who grieve, and change their pain to joy. Amen*

Thought for the day: No matter where we are, God bids us to pray for those near us.

Brenda Coffman (Illinois)

In Praise of Martha

Read Luke 10:38–42

[Martha] said to him, 'Yes, Lord, I believe that you are the Messiah, the Son of God, the one coming into the world.'
John 11:27 (NRSV)

This verse from John's Gospel shows Martha at her best, with her unhesitating affirmation of her faith in Jesus and his mission. But in the reading from Luke, we see another, perhaps more familiar picture of Martha, when she feels overwhelmed by her many tasks and resentful that she has no help from her sister.

I have always felt some sympathy for Martha and have shared the way she felt then: crushed and frustrated. Jesus spoke to Martha at the crucial moment, gently repeating her name. Whether she liked the answer he gave or not, the sound of his voice must surely have made her pause, and her mind become still.

We cannot hear Jesus' live voice as Martha did, but words can bring us stillness in the midst of anger and frustration. I have found the Jesus Prayer—'Lord Jesus Christ, Son of God, have mercy on me, a sinner'—repeated again and again, helps me. Or I might simply pray, 'Lord, help me.' I know, though, that the long-term solution can only come from seeking Mary's 'better part'. She accepted the spiritual food that Jesus offered. We have that food in the Bible, in our prayers and in the guidance of the Holy Spirit. My trust is that in time there will be a stillness in some part of me that remains unshaken, whatever the crisis.

Prayer: *Dear Lord, help me to hear your quiet voice through all the noisy clamour of life, and to act on it. Amen*

Thought for the day: 'Be still and know that I am God' (Psalm 46:10).

Margaret Gregory (Hertfordshire, England)

'The Day of Small Things'

Read Ecclesiastes 3:1–13

Who despises the day of small things?
Zechariah 4:10 (NIV)

'Mum! I'm bored!' This exclamation came from my twelve-year-old son just two weeks into his summer holiday. He would certainly be one answer to the question posed by the prophet Zechariah: 'Who has despised the day of small things?'

Frankly, any of us can become bored with the mundane. To me, the days 'of small things' are those when nothing out of the ordinary happens. We may yearn for excitement, but we would do well to learn to appreciate days when nothing unusual occurs—days of small things. In the course of my life, I have seen some difficult days when people I loved were hurt or died. If I could choose between living these days and ordinary ones, I'd take the ordinary ones every time.

We can decide to appreciate mornings when we wake up to nothing unusual, to nothing beyond the ordinary. We go to work, come home, eat dinner, maybe participate in church activities or help children with homework. Then we settle into bed for a good night's sleep in the home God has provided for us. On those nights, we can remember to thank our extraordinary God who has walked with us through another ordinary day.

Prayer: *Dear Father, we thank you for all of the ordinary days in our lives. Teach us to live each of them for you. In Christ's name. Amen*

Thought for the day: Thank God for every ordinary day.

Harriet Michael (Kentucky)

Friendship with God

Read Psalm 139:1–18

How weighty to me are your thoughts, O God! How vast is the sum of them! I try to count them—they are more than the sand.
Psalm 139:17–18 (NRSV)

My friend and I often go to concerts and the theatre together or meet up for coffee in a cafe. We love to talk. We tell each other our news, our plans, our sorrows and our problems. The time we spend together enriches us as individuals and also enables us to get to know each other better. My knowledge of the needs, interests and desires of my friend allows me to give him presents that please him and are helpful to him. When I see his reaction, I rejoice that I was able to choose the right present.

My experience with this friend reminds me that God knows us much better than we know one another. God knows when we lie down and when we get up. Sometimes we do not even need to articulate our desires or needs; God already knows. God knows us perfectly! And if we are able to give one another thoughtful and appropriate presents, then how much more thoughtful and appropriate are the presents God gives us! Everything good in our lives comes from our friendship with God. Our daily fellowship with our Lord enriches and directs us and draws us closer to God's promises.

Prayer: *Dear Lord, thank you for being our friend. May the time we spend with you be joyful, enriching and transforming. Amen*

Thought for the day: Friendship with God is our highest calling.

Irina Ivanova (Pskov, Russia)

Our Daily Bread

Read Matthew 6:25–34

'Do not keep striving for what you are to eat and what you are to drink, and do not keep worrying.'
Luke 12:29 (NRSV)

My husband's job involves transporting timber to the sawmill. Recently, many days of rain had turned the road leading to the sawmill into mud, making it impossible to drive on. We had been living from day to day, and our money and food were running out.

I remember my anguish as I thought about our children. In my anxiety, a passage from the Gospel of Luke quieted me and brought me inner calm, reminding me that God was well aware of our situation. I gathered the family, and we sat around the bare table. I offered a prayer and gave thanks to God. Five minutes later, the doorbell rang. It was a neighbour whom we did not really know because we had just recently moved into the area. She brought an enormous gift of food. She explained that she had invited a great number of people over that day but that few people had come because of the weather. 'Would you be offended if I shared this food with you, since it is just too much for us?' she asked.

I felt as if I were living the story of Jesus multiplying the loaves and fishes for his followers. The gift of food we received was like the twelve baskets the disciples collected. The food our neighbour gave us sustained us until my husband was able to resume his work. God is always aware of our needs, and sometimes God's faithful and loving response comes in amazing ways.

Prayer: *Thank you, gracious God, for the food you provide every day and for your great love that increases the little that we have. Amen*

Thought for the day: Because God is faithful, we need not be afraid.

Neri Ruth Gattinoni (Buenos Aires, Argentina)

Reluctant Servant

Read Luke 11:5–10

As God's chosen people, holy and dearly loved, clothe yourselves with compassion, kindness, humility, gentleness and patience.
Colossians 3:12 (NIV)

The phone rang as I was leaving home to go to the gym. A friend was ill and she asked me to drive to her house, pick up some flowers and deliver them for her. I thought of the plans I had for my day. Couldn't someone else help her out? Maybe someone who was less busy than me? I thought of excuses—lots of excuses. Then I began to think about how our society prides itself on keeping busy. I keep busy, although I'm retired now and could relax more. I like to stay active.

As I was driving to my friend's home, I prayed for God to help me change my attitude and make me a more cheerful friend. Gradually, I could feel the tension fading from my body, and peace replaced my reluctance. By the time I had completed the short drive, I was feeling glad about the favour I was about to do.

We don't have to be far from home serving on a mission field to help others. God offers us little opportunities every day to serve someone else in some way. I pray that God will open my eyes to little acts of kindness that I can do here and now, and give me a loving heart so that I happily serve.

Prayer: *Dear loving God, open our eyes to opportunities for serving you through helping someone else. Give us courage when we are shy and thoughtfulness when we think we are too busy to help someone in need. Amen*

Thought for the Day: We can be God's hands and feet for someone today.

Phyllis S. Church (Kentucky)

Problem or Possibility?

Read Romans 8:35–39
The gracious hand of our God is on everyone who looks to him.
Ezra 8:22 (NIV)

One morning after a violent autumn storm, I awoke to find a large tree fallen in our garden. Standing at the kitchen window, I surveyed the scene with dismay. 'All that work,' I thought, as I contemplated clearing up the mess. My husband came into the room and stood next to me at the window. 'Look at all that firewood!' he exulted. I was immediately struck by our differing points of view. While I saw the tree only in terms of the mess and damage it had created, my husband looked ahead to winter nights by a warm, crackling fire. I saw a disaster; he saw a blessing.

When faced with unexpected trials, many of us can be so over-whelmed by the immediacy of the problem that we are unable to foresee any possible benefit or good outcome. However, as Christians, we can turn to the many passages in the Bible which remind us that God cares for us and desires good for us, even in the midst of trials. Where the physical eye sees challenges, the eye of faith sees possibilities.

Later, our son and son-in-law helped my husband cut, split and stack the firewood. When we all sat down to enjoy a meal together, the fallen tree didn't seem like such a huge problem. In much the same way, amid the trials of our lives, our faith can give us a new perspective.

Prayer: *O God of comfort, when trials come, help us to remember that you care about us and want to bless us and help us. Amen*

Thought for the day: Every ending can be the start of a new beginning.

DeVonna R. Allison (Michigan)

PRAYER FOCUS: THOSE CLEANING UP A MESS

Kingdom Grace

Read Luke 11:1–4
'Our Father in heaven… Your kingdom come, your will be done on earth as it is in heaven.'
Matthew 6:10 (NIV)

One of my favourite parts of morning worship is praying the Lord's Prayer with the congregation. Praying to invite God's kingdom to come and God's will to be done here on earth is particularly meaningful to me—especially hearing hundreds of people express their desire for God to rule in their lives. When I pray that prayer, as I do almost every day, I remember my need to resubmit my will to God's will each day. Though it is a struggle sometimes for me to make time to tune my will to God's, I have found that such a time of prayer is vital each morning as I face the challenges of a new day.

Even so, I am chagrined by the number of times I fail to follow my intentions to align my will to God's will. But I also know that part of God's provision of 'daily bread' is forgiveness and strength to resist temptation. And every day I experience God's willingness to let me begin again—no matter how many times I fail. So while Jesus' prayer serves as a model for how to pray, it also serves as a conduit of God's grace into my life.

Prayer: *Lord, we want your kingdom to rule, but we often fail to do your will. Thank you for your grace that lets us begin again and again. We pray, 'Our Father in heaven, hallowed be your name, your kingdom come, your will be done on earth as it is in heaven. Give us today our daily bread. Forgive us our debts, as we also have forgiven our debtors. And lead us not into temptation, but deliver us from the evil one.'* *

Thought for the day: In the face of our failures, God provides grace to begin again.

K. Jackson Peevy (Alabama)

* Matthew 6:9–13 (NIV)

By my Side

Read Psalm 119:145–154

Be strong and courageous. Do not be terrified; do not be discouraged, for the Lord your God will be with you wherever you go.
Joshua 1:9 (NIV)

'Mum, come here! Mum!'

The frantic cries of a four-year-old wake me in the darkness. Bleary-eyed, I hurry to our son's room. He's had a bad dream, and now he can't sleep. Speaking softly, I try to ease his fears. Then I lie on the floor beside his bed until he is resting peacefully once more.

I can empathise with my son. I know about not sleeping. My mind races with worries of the day, struggles with my faith, concerns about my family, anxiety about what might happen. These concerns rob me of peace and rest. Only through God's word have I begun to release my anxieties.

Like my son, I seek words of reassurance, and I want to know that my loving parent—my heavenly Father—is by my side. Psalm 23 and Joshua 1:9 remind me that God is with me, leading me, even in the darkest hour. When my soul cries out in the darkness, God's words comfort me and help me to let go of my fears. I can wake in the morning refreshed.

Prayer: *Dear heavenly Father, thank you for your holy word and for your promise to be with us always. Hear our cries, and grant us peace and needed rest. In Jesus' name. Amen*

Thought for the day: How do I sense God's presence in my life?

Jody Suiter (Kansas)

Generous Grace

Read 2 Corinthians 8:1–7

We want you to know, brothers and sisters, about the grace of God that has been granted to the churches of Macedonia; for during a severe ordeal of affliction, their abundant joy and their extreme poverty have overflowed in a wealth of generosity on their part.
2 Corinthians 8:1–2 (NRSV)

It was the day after Christmas, and I had to go to work. I thought that it was going to be a routine day. But just before my lunch break, some of my colleagues and I were called into the Personnel office. Our manager announced to us that another wave of people was being laid off—and we were that wave. When I arrived home, I told my wife the news. She and I then turned to God and asked, 'What now, Lord?' God answered us with a challenge to trust, and faithfully to continue in a lifestyle of generosity.

For us, a lifestyle of generosity is about faithfulness in our giving and being prepared to give as new opportunities arise. My wife and I have committed to continue tithing to our church as well as giving monthly to support an orphan in Ethiopia. We are also giving to some young people in our church who are going on a short-term mission trip to Japan. In addition, we have had the opportunity to give to those in need in our home Bible study. By giving faithfully to meet the needs around us, even in the midst of job loss and a challenging economy, we hope to be like the Macedonian Christians who found grace from God to live a lifestyle of generosity.

Prayer: *Dear God, grant us the grace to give generously even during our most severe trials. Amen*

Thought for the day: Generosity is a way of life that goes beyond money.

Gabriel Forsyth (Florida)

More than an Umbrella

Read Psalm 61:1–5

[The Lord] will cover you with his pinions, and under his wings you will find refuge.
Psalm 91:4 (NRSV)

One spring day I was taking my early morning walk along my usual path. Showers were forecast for the day, so I had my umbrella with me. After I had been walking for a while, the rain began, a light shower at first and then a drenching downpour. Almost everyone ran for cover. I continued my walk, along with a couple of other brave souls, umbrellas in hand as the water splashed around our feet.

I began to understand how, in a similar way, we walk through life sheltered by God's wings. We certainly feel the burdens of life's storms; our path is often like an obstacle course of troubles. But throughout our journey, we can be confident that God will always be with us.

Prayer: *Dear loving God, in our journey through life, shield and protect each of your children. We pray in trust, as Christ taught us, 'Our Father which art in heaven, Hallowed be thy name. Thy kingdom come. Thy will be done, as in heaven, so in earth. Give us day by day our daily bread. And forgive us our sins; for we also forgive every one that is indebted to us. And lead us not into temptation; but deliver us from evil.'* Amen*

Thought for the day: God splashes through life's puddles close beside me.

José M. Semidey Antonetti (Puerto Rico)

* Luke 11:2–4 (KJV)

Productive Plants

Read 1 Corinthians 3:1–9

The one who plants and the one who waters have a common purpose, and each will receive wages according to the labour of each.
1 Corinthians 3:8 (NRSV)

Each spring I plant 50 tomato plants. Typically I use small plants, but I also buy some of the larger, more mature plants so I can enjoy eating fresh tomatoes sooner. However, I know that although I put the 50 tomato plants in the ground, a few of the plants won't grow at all. Early in my gardening years I would pull these plants up, toss them aside, and plant others in their place. One year, instead of discarding these plants, I decided to move them to another area in my garden. Since then, I have been amazed how these small plants often grow bigger and taller than all the other tomato plants in the garden, once I move them.

This annual practice reminds me of God's unending love for us. God gives each of us the ability to grow into productive believers, even if we don't grow very much when our faith is young. I am thankful that we are given the chance to love God and to know that God never gives up on us. Likewise, we can be like God and not give up on others if they too seem not to be growing in their own relationship with God.

Prayer: *Thank you, God, for Jesus. Thank you for the knowledge and understanding you have given each of us. Help us look for ways to encourage those around us as they grow at their own pace. Amen*

Thought for the day: God never, ever gives up on us.

George David McIntosh (Arkansas)

The Trials in our Lives

Read James 1:2–12
Do not be anxious about anything, but in everything, by prayer and petition, with thanksgiving, present your requests to God.
Philippians 4:6 (NIV)

After my third child was born, I was overwhelmed by emotions. I felt blessed to have three healthy boys and a loving husband, but I couldn't shake off the feeling of sadness. Was it baby blues? Lack of sleep? Months later, after sadness had become desperation, my doctor sent me to hospital.

I was humiliated, frustrated and mad at the world, but I lay in my sterile room with no tears to cry. I clung to my Bible, not wanting to let it go but also not having the strength to open it. A nurse came in. She sat next to my bed where I lay in a foetal position. I couldn't look at her. She quietly took the Bible out of my hands and opened it.

'Do not be anxious about anything,' she read from Philippians. As she continued reading, my heart calmed and my soul opened up. We sat and cried together. For the first time in months, I felt the pain, shame and depression lift from my shoulders.

I keep that Bible text pinned up in my bathroom and read it every morning. That nurse helped set me on a path to recovery. She touched my heart and helped my soul to heal by reading the word of God to me.

Prayer: *Dear God, thank you for those who come to us in times of trials with your comfort. Bless those who speak your words of hope and healing. Amen*

Thought for the day: In every dark place, look for light from God.

Whitney Wideman (Georgia)

What's your Food?

I recently overheard a wise woman advising her young-adult child, 'Son, don't let your feelings control your life.' He responded sadly, 'My life is controlling my feelings.' This young man had been desperately looking for work and had announced that although he loved his family and felt their love, life in general had no meaning for him.

People who live in cultures that measure success by occupation and status pass on the ideal to their children early. Children learn to answer the question, 'What do you want to be when you grow up?' Young adults ask, 'Who am I?' and, 'What am I here for?' For those who are middle-aged, the question may be, 'Am I making a contribution?' For older adults: 'How can I make a difference now?' The questions might grow less positive, as in 'What do I have to live for?'

Our circumstances can add to the struggle. They might seem overwhelming, such as enduring difficult illness, living through natural disaster or surviving severe economic upheaval. These situations threaten to steal more than family livelihood and good health; hard times can threaten both our dignity and our sense of purpose.

The underlying question about worth and purpose is not new. Jesus addressed it in a discussion with his disciples (John 4). He had just had an encounter with a woman at a well. He offered her 'living water' to quench her spiritual thirst, that aching for personal worth and purpose. She went away so invigorated and hopeful that she could not keep the story of her change to herself. But just when Jesus had promised quenching of thirst to the woman, his disciples asked him about satisfying hunger. To be fair, they were looking after his welfare when they said, 'Rabbi, eat something.'

He responded, 'I have food to eat that you do not know about. My food is to do the will of him who sent me and to complete his work' (John 4:31, 34). Jesus wasn't speaking only for himself. His sustenance and strength came from doing God's will, but he was encouraging his followers also to find their strength and sustenance from doing the will of God. When we begin to focus on the will of God, we seek a sense of our eternal worth, purpose, meaning and strength. So how do we begin to discover God's will? When Jesus was asked, 'What is the greatest commandment?' and when he was asked, 'What must I do to get eternal life?' he gave the same answer: 'Love God with everything in you, and love your neighbour as yourself' (see Matthew 22:34–39). This single response to two questions tells us how we can find the will of God. We pursue our love of God and love of others through the study of scripture, through continual prayer and through interaction with those who can feed our faith. We live by serving others, by sharing our Christ-experiences with others, by following Christ in showing grace to others.

Still, whether we are with family or friends at work, at play or even worshipping, life may seem a chain of random events with little meaning. Some people may feel sure of the worth and meaning of life in general but baffled by the question of their own personal meaning and purpose. To them Jesus says, 'God does have a purpose for your life.' He goes on to remind the disciples that, although God is up to something generally in the world, there are specific purposes for each of us: 'For here the saying holds true, "One sows and another reaps." I sent you to reap that for which you did not labour. Others have laboured, and you have entered into their labour.'

Though the call to love is direct and general, how we pursue that calling is specific to each of us. We may find our specific purpose by asking others what they see as our strengths. They might see buds of 'eternal fruit' in our interaction with family and friends. We may live God's purpose for us in our employment, but it may also be completely separate from our occupation. Even so, our purpose and sense of worth, and the eternal fruit God is growing through our lives, will be reflected in how we do our work and relate to others.

According to Jesus, our ultimate sustenance comes from connecting to God's will for the world as well as to God's will for our own lives. This will is focused on finding ways to love God and love others. We can do this in the midst of joy and suffering, with understanding and mystery, with peace and in spite of our struggle. And God walks with us.

In many of the meditations in this issue the writers point to the search for deeper meaning and finding purpose, often by persisting through tough circumstances. In others, the writers recount their struggles to name and use their specific gifts to make a difference in the world.

You may want to re-read the meditations for January 1, 3, 6, 12, 15, 25, and 29; for February 1, 4, 9, 10, 11, 15, 17, 25 and 27; for March 12 and 20; and for April 6 and 13 as you consider the questions below.

Questions for Reflection

1. If your 'food is to do the will of God', what comes to mind for you to do?

2. What keeps you loving God and loving others? Who do you see clearly loving God and loving others? How can you join with them in that?

3. Who has helped you to identify your strengths and gifts? Have you been told about your unique gifts for the world? If so, what have you been told?

4. What needs and causes in your community draw your interest or concern? What situations in your nation tug at your mind and heart? What situations in the world? What steps can you take to work in those areas?

5. What activities give you great satisfaction? How do you see those activities connecting with God's purposes? Should they?

6. What scripture passages speak to you about your personal worth or about your purpose in life?

7. Where do you find 'living water' to quench your spiritual thirst?

Tony Peterson (Nashville, Tennessee)

Tony Peterson is a Christian educator and freelance writer/editor, who currently teaches young children in an after-school ministry. He and his wife, Laura, enjoy spending time with their six children and six grandchildren.

Emmanuel—God with Us

Read Psalm 23

Even though I walk through the valley of the shadow of death, I will fear no evil, for you are with me.
Psalm 23:4 (NIV)

My two young adult children have cystic fibrosis, and a few years ago, when my daughter was 17 years old, she had a successful double lung transplant. For the whole year prior to her transplant she had been dying a slow death. Every day we had to be prepared that it could be her last day here on Earth.

In human terms the heartbreaking trauma of that year threatened to overwhelm us, physically, mentally and emotionally. It was our faith that helped to give us a different perspective to the trials we were going through. I was amazed by God's continuous provision for us. He strengthened us for each step in the present while he also prepared the future steps for us. He listened patiently to our doubts and calmed our fears. He gave us hope in our hopelessness and helped us to surrender the situation to him, whatever the outcome, by reassuring us of the hope of heaven. And he used our story to touch the lives of others.

Prayer: *Father, in our times of trial, when we are exhausted and have doubts and questions, please open our eyes so that we can see how close you are to us. Thank you that you never leave us, but instead walk with us each step of the way. Amen*

Thought for the day: God walks with us through every day of our lives.

Helen Little (Dublin, Ireland)

'Let's Pray'

Read Hebrews 11:1–16
If you have faith as small as a mustard seed, you can say to this mountain, 'Move from here to there' and it will move. Nothing will be impossible for you.
Matthew 17:20 (NIV)

Aunt Marion had eight children and a large extended family. She was the one we all telephoned when we had a difficulty or concern or wanted to share some good news. One of the many things I loved about her was that whenever I called her with a problem, at some point she would say, 'Let's pray.' And then we would do just that. Aunt Marion believed God. The Bible says that praying makes a big difference (James 5:16); Aunt Marion knew that is true and that we can count on it.

Hers was a good example of faith. Every morning found her seated at the kitchen table with her Bible, a daily devotional and her journal. Most of her journal pages were filled not with accounts of the worries and woes of life but with Bible texts she had written out to address every situation she faced.

Faith is not tangible. But one way to have faith is to act on the truth of God's word. That can make our faith visible. In challenging circumstances, instead of focusing on the problem or the worry, I can read God's word, remember it and think about its truth—something that never changes. God can help us use even a tiny amount of faith to move mountains.

Prayer: *Dear Lord, help us to read your word and to remember what you have to say about the problems we face. Amen*

Thought for the day: Reading the Bible offers us truth and strength.

Juanita Davies (New Jersey)

The Gift of New Life

Read John 11:28–45

[Mary] said to him… 'Lord, if you had been here, my brother would not have died.'
John 11:32 (NRSV)

If only God had acted, we would not have had to face some of our own problems. It is tempting to blame our difficulties on God's slowness to act. When Jesus began to weep over the death of Lazarus, someone said, 'Could not he who opened the eyes of the blind man have kept this man from dying?' Could not God have prevented trouble from coming into our lives? If God loves us, why do we suffer?

For the sake of the crowd standing around, we are told, Jesus prayed and then shouted in front of the tomb, 'Lazarus, come out!' Lazarus emerged, his hands and feet and face wrapped in cloth. He found new life but was still bound until others, at Jesus' command, unbound him.

God acts constantly and mercifully in our lives, though often our insensitivity keeps us from seeing it. Removing the 'cloths' from our eyes requires paying close attention, looking for God's presence and action even when it seems as if nothing is happening.

We may ask and expect God to act in spectacular ways, but spiritual maturity sees God at work in the ordinary, the mundane, the routine aspects of our lives. When we can see that, we can experience the new life that Christ brings.

Prayer: *O God, forgive our accusations that you ignore us, and open our eyes to your presence and mercy. May we help to unbind others so they see the new life you offer. Amen*

Thought for the day: Today, look for God's presence in every situation.

William O. Paulsell (Kentucky)

PRAYER FOCUS: THOSE MOURNING A RECENT DEATH

Good Deeds

Read Hebrews 10:19–25

Let us consider how to provoke one another to love and good deeds.
Hebrews 10:24 (NRSV)

My friend Tom recently moved to Guatemala as a missionary. Tom serves in a small, remote village, where he oversees a health clinic that helps women and children, especially, who struggle with despair, sickness and malnutrition.

Some months after Tom moved, he sent me a small supply of prayer bracelets—small, cloth bands that the women of the village had made. I tied one of these bands around my wrist so that I would remember to pray for Tom's work and for the people of Guatemala. Every time I looked at the band or became aware of it on my wrist, I whispered a prayer, asking that Tom would be encouraged and that his good work would continue.

I've prayed for Tom and the people of Guatemala while I was in some interesting places—while watching a football match, driving my car and drinking a morning cup of coffee. What I've learned is this: our prayers don't have to be flowery or lengthy. Our prayers for others can encourage them to continue in the good work God has set before them.

Prayer: *Dear God, please bless the good work of our families, friends and congregation. Bless all who serve you in remote places and lift up those who are discouraged and faint-hearted. Amen*

Thought for the day: Today, where can I encourage others as they serve?

Todd Outcalt (Indiana)

From Performance to Passion

Read Psalm 150

Sing to [the Lord] a new song; play skilfully on the strings, with loud shouts.

Psalm 33:3 (NRSV)

During my school years, my life was devoted to playing the violin. I played in the school orchestra by day and practised at home by night. My summers were spent on music courses or in the orchestra pit rehearsing for local theatre productions. So it was somewhat surprising that when I left school, I put my instrument down, seemingly for good. I had grown tired of the constant practice required just to earn a more prominent place in the violin section or a better score in the next competition. I didn't pick up the violin again until almost 15 years later, when our church was looking for musicians to play in a worship group. Surprisingly, playing was a totally different experience this time. Using my instrument to express my love and passion for God made playing the violin a joy instead of a job.

Often we approach what we do for God the way I initially played the violin, with emphasis on performance. We become so focused on the outcome of our efforts that we lose the simple joy of serving God to the best of our abilities with the gifts given us. When we allow the passion in our hearts to motivate us rather than seeking human approval, what we do can truly bring glory to the God we serve.

Prayer: *Dear Father, thank you for the opportunity to worship you with the gifts you have given us. May we offer all we do out of passion for you.*

Thought for the day: Serving God is meant to be a joy, not a job.

Link2Life: *Look for a way to use an old skill in your church.*

Elaine L. Bridge (Ohio)

A Clean Slate

Read Luke 15:11–32
If anyone is in Christ, there is a new creation: everything old has passed away; see, everything has become new!
2 Corinthians 5:17 (NRSV)

My colleague told of a dream whereby he came to feel the forgiveness of God. In this dream, he told God that he wished to be forgiven for the wrongs he had done. God responded by asking him to list his transgressions on a blackboard. He started writing a list of what he considered to be 'minor sins'. To his surprise, as rapidly as he wrote, God erased the words. Amazed, my friend wondered what would happen with more 'major' sins. He began to add what he thought to be more serious offences. Almost in disbelief, he saw the same erasing action occur. No matter what he wrote, God quickly erased it.

Waking from the dream, he thought of the Bible verse above about becoming a new creation and about God's love being like that of the prodigal's loving father. My friend believes that God welcomes us and erases our transgressions just as he saw in the dream.

We can confess all misdeeds and sins, both large and small, ask for forgiveness, and know that God not only forgives but also erases our sins as if they had never existed. With our slate wiped clean, we are new creations.

Prayer: *Make us as willing to come to you, O Lord, as you are to receive us. Embrace us. As your prodigals come home, Lord, forgive us and hold us in your love, now and for ever. Amen*

Thought for the day: God promises to remember our sin no more (see Jeremiah 31:33–34).

William Louis Dike (Florida)

Blind Spots

Read 1 Corinthians 8:1–13

Be careful, however, that the exercise of your freedom does not become a stumbling block to the weak.
1 Corinthians 8:9 (NIV)

As a result of eye surgery, I have a blind spot that affects the vision in my left eye. While this is not generally a problem, I need to be careful while driving and use particular caution when merging to the left into traffic.

Of course, I realise that other drivers are not aware of my impaired vision; they don't know that I can't see them as soon as other drivers might. Therefore, to expect them to give me more leeway than they do other drivers would be dangerous.

I see a spiritual parallel to my physical infirmity. We do not always know the spiritual limitations of others. A friend might suggest doing something that because of my spiritual weakness could harm me, though it would not be a problem for my friend. I have to exercise discernment and proceed with caution in areas where I know I am weak.

Similarly, I want to be sensitive to the 'blind spots' of others. When a friend says no to something I suggest, I can accept that with understanding, not judging but rejoicing that my friend is responding to God's direction.

Prayer: *Loving God, help us to encourage one another to follow your guidance so that we may grow spiritually stronger every day. Amen*

Thought for the day: My way to follow God is uniquely different from others' paths.

Lisa Stackpole (Wisconsin)

PRAYER FOCUS: PEOPLE WITH IMPAIRED VISION

Live for Christ

Read Philippians 2:1–8

Remember your leaders, those who spoke the word of God to you; consider the outcome of their way of life, and imitate their faith.
Hebrews 13:7 (NRSV)

Without a doubt, the death of a loved one is one of life's most difficult experiences. The pain and emptiness are indescribable. Yet somehow this experience allows us to reflect not only on the life of our loved one but on our life as well.

A few months ago my uncle died. During the funeral service, people told stories about my uncle's character, his home life, his work and his tireless efforts for the church. We learned details of his life and work that we had never known. His was a fine example of a life lived imitating Christ, and today we see the fruits of his work in the legacy he left.

Jesus Christ left a great legacy for us in his life, death and resurrection. We have his story of God's love and forgiveness to tell the world. As we tell Christ's story, our lives can reflect his life. What stories will people tell about us when we are gone? How will our legacy honour Christ?

Prayer: *O Lord, help us to remember daily your great love for us and to proclaim it by our actions for all to hear. Amen*

Thought for the day: How do I reflect Christ in my life?

Eva Ferrer (Carolina, Puerto Rico)

No More Manna

Read Joshua 5:9–12

On the day after the passover, on that very day, they ate the produce of the land, unleavened cakes and parched grain. The manna ceased.
Joshua 5:11–12 (NRSV)

For 40 years in the desert, God's people were assured they would not go hungry. But they could—and did—grow weary of their monotonous diet of manna. Then, once they crossed the Jordan into the promised land, the manna ceased—no more guaranteed food. God's people had the freedom to fail, but they also had the faith that could help them succeed. Perhaps that's why they marked crossing the river by celebrating Passover, eating the unleavened bread.

Our 40 days of Lent can be a reminder of the Hebrews' 40 years in the desert. Our Christian rituals that involve fasting instead of feasting can sometimes seem drab and dreary. Still, we are assured we will get through them through reflection and confession. And our meal of hope, the bread and cup, symbolises the faith that equips us to answer Christ's call. Beyond the slavery of sin lies the freedom of the resurrection. That is the promised land that awaits us. When we share the bread and cup, we experience a small taste of resurrection. This is not a drab meal!

Prayer: *Living Christ, dwell with us on our journey of faith, and never let us take you for granted. Amen*

Thought for the day: Jesus is the bread of life.

Frank Ramirez (Pennsylvania)

Do Not Lose Heart

Read Philippians 3:12–16

Do not fear, for I am with you, do not be afraid, for I am your God.
Isaiah 41:10 (NRSV)

My husband and I went to see our six-year-old granddaughter participate in a school sports' competition. One of the events was the 100-yard race.

Some of the youngsters, including my granddaughter, did not reach the goal or receive a prize because they were constantly looking back rather than concentrating on pushing forward. They were thrown off course, the ground they had gained on those behind them was lost, and they did not reach the goal.

The same thing happens in our spiritual life when we constantly look back and become preoccupied with mistakes of the past. Holding on to memories of past sins can cause us to lose heart and we do not reach our objective. Paul reminds us in Philippians to leave the past behind and look forward to what lies ahead in order to attain 'the prize of the heavenly call of God in Christ Jesus' (Philippians 3:14).

Prayer: *Loving God, help us continue without looking back, to move ahead toward the goal of God's calling in Jesus Christ, who taught us to pray, 'Our Father in heaven, hallowed be your name, your kingdom come, your will be done on earth as it is in heaven. Give us today our daily bread. Forgive us our debts, as we also have forgiven our debtors. And lead us not into temptation, but deliver us from the evil one.'* Amen*

Thought for the day: Life in Christ releases us from the past.

Elba I. González (Carolina, Puerto Rico)

* Matthew 6:9–13 (NIV)

Reflections

Read John 1:1–5

The Son is the radiance of God's glory and the exact representation of his being.
Hebrews 1:3 (NIV)

On a clear and windless day, a smooth lake can reflect an almost perfect mirror image of the landscape around it—often creating scenes of stunning beauty.

Jesus Christ is more than a reflection; he is the exact representation of God. As we read stories about Jesus' earthly ministry—how he taught and healed and ultimately died for us—we are prone to lose sight of that most important truth; Jesus *is* God (John 1:1). When we look at Christ, we see who God is and what he does.

Christ, who stepped out of the realms of glory in heaven to reach out to each of us, is the very God who created the universe. Not only did the Living Word create the cosmos (John 1:3; Colossians 1:16), but Christ also sustains and holds the creation together (Colossians 1:17). And yet this all-powerful Creator loves each of us personally and individually and bids us come close.

Every time we see beauty reflected, we can think of and give thanks for Christ, the exact representation of God. And yet he is much more than a reflection. When Jesus said, 'I and the Father are one' (John 10:30), that is exactly what he meant.

Prayer: *Dear Heavenly Father, thank you that your Son reflects your love and compassion for each of us. Help us to reflect your nature to those you place in our path. Amen*

Thought for the day: When we are like Jesus, we show God to the world.

Michael J. Reynolds (Florida)

By Design

Read Psalm 139:1–16

In him we were… chosen, having been predestined according to the plan of him who works out everything in conformity with… his will, in order that we… might be for the praise of his glory.
Ephesians 1:11–12 (NIV)

Being made redundant gave me the opportunity to reflect on what God's purpose for my life may be. I remembered reading how God had provided shelter, food, clothing and education for thousands of orphaned children over a period of 62 years, simply through the prayers and leadership of one man, George Müller. He was convinced that God had selected him for this work, even before his birth.

Checking this out as a biblical truth made me think of people like Moses, Joseph, Gideon, Esther, even Jesus; those whom God certainly seemed to have designed, created and positioned to fulfil his specific purposes for their lives. Having watched amazed as my children's lives unfold, I ponder on each of our God-given gifts and talents, and the different circumstances he knows we will face.

God has designed each of us for the work he has planned for us in our lives, too. Maybe it's more obvious when we look at the lives of biblical characters in hindsight, but our 'callings' are just as valid, and we too are integral to God's plans.

Prayer: *Father God, I am honoured that you made me for your glory. I give myself afresh to you today for the fulfilment of your purposes. Help me, please, to listen for your direction for my life. Amen*

Thought for the day: In what circumstances do I find myself, and what contribution can I make?

M.S. Foster (Cheshire, England)

Don't forget to renew your annual subscription to *The Upper Room*! If you enjoy the notes, why not also consider giving a gift subscription to a friend or member of your family?

You will find a subscription order form overleaf.

The Upper Room is also available from your local Christian bookshop.

Individual Subscriptions

☐ I would like to take out a subscription myself (complete your name and address details only once)

☐ I would like to give a gift subscription (please complete both name and address sections below)

Your name..

Your address..

....Postcode..

Gift subscription name..

Gift subscription address..

....Postcode..

Gift message (20 words max)..

....

Please send *The Upper Room* beginning with the May 2011 / September 2011 / January 2012 issue: (delete as applicable)

THE UPPER ROOM ☐ £13.80

Please complete the payment details below and send, with appropriate payment, to: BRF, 15 The Chambers, Vineyard, Abingdon OX14 3FE

Total enclosed £.......... (cheques should be made payable to 'BRF')

Payment by ☐ cheque ☐ postal order ☐ Visa ☐ Mastercard ☐ Switch

Card no: ☐☐☐☐ ☐☐☐☐ ☐☐☐☐ ☐☐☐☐ ☐☐☐☐ ☐☐☐☐

Expires: ☐☐☐☐ Security code: ☐☐☐

Issue no (Switch): ☐☐☐☐

Signature (essential if paying by credit/Switch card) ....

☐ Please do not send me further information about BRF publications

☐ Please send me a Bible reading resources pack to encourage Bible reading in my church

BRF is a Registered Charity

Encouraging Words

Read Romans 12:1–13
Encourage one another and build up each other.
1 Thessalonians 5:11 (NRSV)

On a steamy, hot Florida afternoon, I sat waiting for my car to be repaired. I was tired, overwhelmed and discouraged. I had recently moved across the country to take my first teaching position in an inner-city elementary school. The new job was challenging, and I was questioning whether the move had been a wise one. I decided to mark a few maths homework papers as I waited.

Moments later, I heard a voice saying, 'You must be a school teacher.'

I looked up to see the warm smile of an elderly man. He told me how much he appreciated all the hard work teachers do. Then he said, 'I want to buy you a cold drink while you wait for your car.'

As I sipped the cold drink he bought for me, I felt a difference in my attitude and my outlook. The kind, supportive words of a stranger had encouraged me. I know that God used him to help me when I needed my spirits lifted.

Each day, we have opportunities to say words of encouragement. I pray that I won't be too busy, distracted or reticent to do so when I see a chance to make a positive difference in another person's day.

Prayer: *Thank you, God, for your amazing love and for sending people to encourage us when we need it. Help us to be channels of support and encouragement for those around us. Amen*

Thought for the day: Today, be God's messenger of encouragement.

Stephanie J. Hoard (Indiana)

Treasure Seeker

Read Proverbs 2:1–5

Yes, beg for knowledge; plead for insight. Look for it as hard as you would for silver or some hidden treasure.
Proverbs 2:3–4 (GNB)

Our family was panning for gold in a nearby river. We sloshed into the water at the river's edge and positioned the sluice box (a grooved trough used for separating gold from sand and rocks). My husband scooped in a shovelful of mud from the river bottom. Water flooded the box, washing away grains of sand. Dead leaves and twigs floated to the surface. We cleaned out this debris along with larger rocks and pebbles and scoured the bottom of the trough for precious flakes of gold.

As I watched, I realised that we are like soil from the river bottom, worth something but also filled with debris. But when we dig into and apply God's word to everyday circumstances, the Lord filters from our lives what is useless. We seek and God helps us discover treasure in the Bible.

As scripture permeates our hearts and minds, it cleanses us of destructive emotions. Ephesians 4:31–32 tells us how to deal with bitterness and anger. Philippians 4:6 helps us confront anxious thoughts. The Bible offers solutions for attitudes that block us from becoming the people God created us to be. Our lives can shine with substance and lasting value.

Prayer: *Thank you, God, for the priceless treasures you reveal to us as we read the Bible. Amen*

Thought for the day: God builds on the best in us.

Kathleen Kohler (Washington)

A Time to Wait

Read Isaiah 40:26–31
Let the peace of Christ rule in your hearts.
Colossians 3:15 (NRSV)

My wife is quick to remind me that I am not good at waiting. She has often pointed out that I make some situations more difficult by pushing ahead before I have all the facts or the co-operation of others. I don't want to be like that. I believe that the first step in changing our behaviour is awareness. Coming into these and similar situations over and over again can get our attention and help us become aware of attitudes or behaviour that hinder our relationship with God or create problems for others.

When we are dealing with worry, anger, impatience or other signs of anxiety, Christ offers us a sense of peace that can transcend whatever challenge we face. When troubles or situations arise that threaten our peace, we can rely on the strength of our relationship with God by calling on God in prayer and choosing to accept God's peace in place of our anxiety. Remembering Christ's words in John 14 and applying them in our lives helps us to practise our faith when troubles come or when we feel impatient.

Prayer: *Dear God of peace, help us to sense your presence at all times and to seek your peace. Amen*

Thought for the day: Peace comes from knowing that Christ holds all things together (see Colossians 1:17).

Mark H. Anderson (Pennsylvania)

The Extra Mile

Read 2 Corinthians 9:6–15

If anyone forces you to go one mile, go also the second mile.
Matthew 5:41 (NRSV)

A new pizzeria has opened in our part of town. One day I popped in and ordered a pizza and a coffee. I was surprised when the waiter brought me a small dish of chocolates and sweets as well. I hadn't ordered them. They were unexpected and therefore brought me joy. But this was not the end of the surprises. When I asked for the bill, I discovered two chocolate mints on the plate with my receipt. The staff of the pizzeria do not restrict themselves to carrying out their duties but also attend to their customers in other ways.

These kindnesses caused me to think about how Christians obey the Bible's commands to serve. We can bring God pleasure when we don't limit ourselves simply to carrying out our task but invest love, concern, attention and diligence. When we apply God's principles in our lives, we allow God's grace to be revealed in and through us. And all over this world, there will be extra smiles; kind words; and unexpected joy, hope and encouragement.

Prayer: *Dear Lord, thank you for your truth revealed to us in your word. Help us not only to know but to apply your word in our lives. Make us instruments of grace. Amen*

Thought for the day: Where can I do more than is expected of me, as an act of love?

Irina Ivanova (Pskov, Russia)

Drowning?

Read Mark 4:35–41

'Woe to me!' [Isaiah] cried. 'I am ruined! For I am a man of unclean lips, and I live among a people of unclean lips, and my eyes have seen the King, the Lord Almighty.'

Isaiah 6:5 (NIV)

While visiting a public swimming pool recently, I considered the contrast between the lifeguard and those who are in danger. Being the lifeguard is by far the more desirable position. I would prefer something like the role of lifeguard in my daily life as well. But the truth is I am often more like the one who is drowning.

I am the one who needs the Lord to provide my daily food, clothing and shelter (Matthew 6:33). I am the one who has sinned and fallen short of God's glory (Romans 3:23). As a result, I am the one in need of daily forgiveness as I confess my sins and my need for God (1 John 1: 9). I am the one drowning. Like Isaiah, I have unclean lips (Isaiah 6:5). Like Paul, I do the very things that I do not want to do (Romans 7:15). Like Peter, I try to help God and act in ways that my human understanding dictates as a better plan (Matthew 16:22; John 18:10–11)—even though I am the one drowning.

Aren't we all more like the one drowning than like the lifeguard? Jesus said, 'Blessed are those who are poor in spirit'—those who recognise their need for God—'for theirs is the kingdom of heaven' (Matthew 5:3). The more we recognise our desperate need for God, the closer we come to God's kingdom.

Prayer: *Dear God, help us to remember when we feel as if we are drowning that you are close at hand to help us. Amen*

Thought for the day: Stop struggling—our Lifeguard is always on duty.

Andy Baker (Tennessee)

PRAYER FOCUS: THOSE WHO FEAR WATER

Spiritual Treasure

Read Isaiah 33:5–6

Store up for yourselves treasures in heaven, where moth and rust do not destroy, and where thieves do not break in and steal. For where your treasure is, there your heart will be also.
Matthew 6:20–21 (NIV)

One morning my husband and I went out for breakfast. When we walked back into our home, we noticed with a sinking feeling that some things seemed out of place. Our home had been burgled.

I couldn't believe it! Within a short time, items that had long been part of my life had been taken from me. I felt devastated by strangers coming into my home and taking my possessions.

Nevertheless, I had to remind myself that despite my sadness at losing things I valued, those items were material and not truly important. My heart's desire is not to store up possessions but to store up the heavenly treasure of knowing and loving God. Relationship with God is my most valued treasure.

Matthew 6 reminds us of our choice. Do we cherish earthly treasure or heavenly treasure? One can be destroyed or stolen; the other goes with us into eternity.

That morning I saw what is most worth keeping—and am I glad I did!

Prayer: *Protector of all who trust, help us to seek you as our true treasure. We pray in Jesus' name. Amen*

Thought for the day: What is my greatest treasure?

Julie White (California)

God Never Leaves our Side

Read John 14:15–26

Jesus said, 'I will not leave you orphaned; I am coming to you.'
John 14:18 (NRSV)

I live in a close-knit family with my elderly parents and a younger sister. My parents are in their 80s. My mother is starting to have knee problems, and my father is in the last stages of emphysema.

For years, I have constantly feared that my father would die soon. My fear is compounded when I think of my future being alone with my sister, who is bipolar. Without the warmth and support of my parents, handling the daily challenges of life will be more difficult. What shall I do if my sister's condition worsens?

All these fears and worries led me to seek help from a psychiatrist. Although medication did help to relieve some of my symptoms of depression and anxiety, the ongoing problem of wondering about my future persisted.

One day as I was reading my Bible, I realised that God was speaking to me through John 14:18. No matter what my age is, I am always a child of God. And when my parents die, God will not abandon me. This promise has given me much comfort and strength.

Now when I take care of my ailing father, I do the best I can and leave the rest in God's hands. No longer do I feel hopeless or fearful of the future. I have found the peace of mind and heart that the Lord offers each one of us.

Prayer: *Dear Lord, help us to release our anxieties to you. In gratitude we place our lives in your loving care. Amen*

Thought for the day: We find peace when we place our present and our future in God's hands.

Doris Yeung (Samutprakam, Thailand)

PRAYER FOCUS: PEOPLE CARING FOR ELDERLY PARENTS

Retired? Not Yet

Read Numbers 8:23–26

Though outwardly we are wasting away, yet inwardly we are being renewed day by day.
2 Corinthians 4:16 (NIV)

I am an octogenarian and considered retired from vocational pursuits. However, the question is, 'Am I, really?' Is a vocation the pursuit of a specific career goal? Or is my lifetime vocation to use my gifts for God's purposes—in which case I will never retire?

Consider the Lord's instructions to Moses concerning the Levites in the reading above (vv. 24–25). The Levites were to begin serving at the age of 25 and retire at the age of 50. Thereafter, they were to continue to assist—just not in their former priestly role. Their role changed to the equally important role of assisting others.

I am considerably older than 50. In fact, I am almost the age 18th-century preacher John Wesley was when he wrote in his journal that he was troubled with severe health problems. Then he added: 'However, blessed be God, I do not slack my labour; I can preach and write still.' I cannot preach, but I can write a little, and I can pray constantly. This is where I belong—persevering into the future, serving God all the way.

Prayer: *Thank you, Lord Jesus, for your invitation, 'Come follow me.' As long as we have breath, may we respond. We pray as you taught us, saying, 'Father, hallowed be your name, your kingdom come. Give us each day our daily bread. Forgive us our sins, for we also forgive everyone who sins against us. And lead us not into temptation.'* * Amen

Thought for the day: There's no mandatory retirement age for serving Christ.

John Eyberg (Oklahoma)

PRAYER FOCUS: THOSE FEELING USELESS
* Luke 11:2–4 (NIV)

Knowing and Loving

Read Psalm 139:1–12
O Lord, you have searched me and known me.
Psalm 139:1 (NRSV)

In a documentary film about an international celebrity, the film's producer explained how he had come to care deeply about the person who was the focus of this work. 'To know anyone is to love them,' he said. Though I'm not sure this is true, I thought of the people dearest to me and realised my knowledge of them is the basis of my love for them. Then I remembered people I had found irritating at first, who became more likeable to me when I knew their stories. I recalled reading about violent criminals, disgraced public figures, even everyday men and women who became caught in their own weaknesses. All had complex stories; but as I learned their individual histories, my anger and judgment softened.

Soon I realised that God's love for me is rooted in a surpassing depth of knowledge about me. God knows my every fault and virtue. God reads the notes of encouragement I write to others, hears the phone calls I make to a lonely housebound person, and sees me help my disabled son make his bed. God also sees me lose patience, hears the hurtful words I say, and knows every foolish choice I have ever made.

In our weaknesses and our strengths, we can trust that God's intimate knowledge of us is inseparable from his enduring love for us.

Prayer: *Loving God, help us to know others so that we may love them. Teach us not to judge but to listen. Amen*

Thought for the day: God sees me at my worst and loves me anyway.

Julia Denton (Virginia)

Lives that Shine

Read Matthew 5:13–16

Always be ready to make your defence to anyone who demands from you an accounting for the hope that is in you; yet do it with gentleness and reverence.
1 Peter 3:15–16 (NRSV)

At the age of 16 I became excited about being a Christian, and I began to explore ways to share my faith. I walked through neighbourhoods at night, leaving gospel tracts on the windscreens of parked cars. A youth magazine printed my testimony, and I wrote letters to people about the doom facing those who rejected God's offer of salvation. Despite my well-intended efforts, I never heard of anyone making a commitment to Christ because of what I did.

Later, while attending a youth camp, I was injured in a car accident. Several campers visited me, and I told them how God was helping me cope with my temporary limitations. After I had returned home, my pastor received a letter from one of the campers. She said that despite growing up in a Christian home, she had never made a profession of faith. 'However, when I saw the joy and peace in Dave's life in spite of his pain, I decided to commit my life to Jesus.'

I hadn't tried to persuade anyone to follow God that day, yet in everyday living, God spoke through me. I learned that while God can use literature and sermons, some people come to faith only when they see a flesh-and-blood example of Christianity in action. Our most effective witnessing may happen when we don't even realise it.

Prayer: *O God, let your love be evident in our lives so that those who are away from you may find their way home. Amen*

Thought for the day: When our lives 'shine for Jesus', others will notice.

David S. McCarthy (South Carolina)

Formed in Us

Read Isaiah 55:1–13

The Lord declares, 'My word that goes out from my mouth… will not return to me empty, but will accomplish what I desire and achieve the purpose for which I sent it.'

Isaiah 55:11 (NIV)

My mother was crying because she could no longer easily recall Bible verses that have energised and informed her life for decades. This was a profound loss for her, and she felt it keenly.

I commiserated. During the previous year, I had committed several psalms to memory. I could recite them perfectly. Three or four months later, they slipped away because I wasn't reciting them every day. As we grieved our losses, I realised that what we learn in our youth can slip away as the brain ages.

Observing our sadness, my father offered words of wisdom. 'The word has not left you,' he said. 'While you were memorising it, the word did its work in you. It has become a part of who you are.' What a helpful comment!

When we interact with the Bible through study and memorising, it works in us and continues to bear fruit throughout our lives—even when we are no longer able to recall its words exactly.

Prayer: *Thank you, Lord, for the influence of your eternal word, which stays with us always. Amen*

Thought for the day: God's message in scripture shapes us and bears fruit in our lives as long as we live.

Link2Life: *Volunteer to read the Bible to someone who has difficulty reading.*

Diane Boleyn (Iowa)

Life of Mission

Read 1 Kings 19:1–18

There came a voice to him that said, 'What are you doing here, Elijah?'
1 Kings 19:13 (NRSV)

In 1 Kings 18 we read how Elijah, the prophet of the Lord, had a contest with the prophets of Baal. The outcome demonstrated that the Lord, not Baal, is the only true God to be worshipped. Suddenly, Elijah flees for fear of his life as Jezebel threatens to kill him. Fear overcomes Elijah, and he forgets both what God has done through him and that he can protect him from Jezebel.

God appears to Elijah and asks him, 'What are you doing here, Elijah?' Elijah pleads with God to take his life because he is the only prophet of the Lord remaining. Possibly Elijah had forgotten, or purposely decided not to accomplish, the mission God wanted him to do.

Sometimes I too find myself in situations when worry and fear overcome me—worry about not having enough money, food, clothes and good health. Fear of not knowing what the future holds, or where I am going to be or of not succeeding in my career can engulf me. These become constant distractions that can divert my attention from my life's mission and what God wants me to do. But as I depend more on God, I worry less and remain focused on what's really important: serving in God's kingdom around me.

Prayer: *Dear God of assurance, train our spiritual eyes to focus on you and our mission in life, for the growth of your kingdom. Amen*

Thought for the day: What does my daily life say about my priorities?

Link2Life: *Put on your calendar an activity that better reflects what you want your priorities to be.*

Philip Polo (Nairobi, Kenya)

Not that Different

Read Colossians 3:11–15

There is one body and one Spirit—just as you were called to one hope when you were called.
Ephesians 4:4 (NIV)

Recently I've been trying to do a better job of keeping in touch with friends and family members. It's nearly ten years since I left college, so I thought it might be nice to catch up with my former roommate. She is also a Christian, and lives in her native country, Malaysia. When this former classmate replied to my email, I was amazed at how similar her situation is to mine. She's married and working to balance her career and family life. She's using the internet to find work-at-home opportunities. She's growing in her relationship with Christ. She's facing the everyday challenges of life—just as I am.

I live, work, shop and worship within a twelve-mile area. I tend to focus on my own world, not remembering my brothers and sisters in Christ around the world. But God's word challenges me to expand my focus. The Bible reminds us that we are all part of the same body and that God is Father of us all. As we try to respond to God's call on our lives, we are not alone. We are surrounded by a great cloud of witnesses in heaven and on earth (Hebrews 12:1). We are united with those who have gone before us in faith and those who are on the journey with us now—no matter where in the world they are.

Prayer: *Dear Lord, help us to remember that we have brothers and sisters all around the world. In Jesus' name. Amen*

Thought for the day: We all face similar challenges, no matter where we live.

Link2Life: *Contact a friend from years past and catch up.*

Lisa Earl (Pennsylvania)

Come as You Are

Read Hebrews 4:14–16

Let us then approach the throne of grace with confidence, so that we may receive mercy and find grace to help us in our time of need.
Hebrews 4:16 (NIV)

I recall from childhood my family being invited to a 'come as you are' party. Guests were to simply come, without worrying about what they might wear or bring. Our actions sometimes show our lack of forethought—we 'just do it'. More often, though, we prepare for all kinds of activities. For example, we wash our hands before meals and complete lengthy to-do lists before going on holiday. We think preparation is always necessary. There are times, nonetheless, when efforts to prepare are unnecessary and also futile.

Jesus invites us to come as we are. 'Impossible!' you might exclaim, 'I'm not ready to present myself to God just as I am.' Incredibly, that is exactly what God wants us to do.

As an act of faith, we set aside our inclination to prepare. In doing so, we acknowledge our inability to prepare ourselves for God's kingdom. God alone can prepare us, forgive us and redeem us. Only when we give ourselves as we are can our lives be transformed through grace to serve and glorify God.

Prayer: *Sovereign God, we come to you just as we are. Remake us into who you would have us be. Amen*

Thought for the day: God has invited us. Let's go just as we are.

Robert L. Stephens (Virginia)

Bread-Making

Read Matthew 13:31–33

Jesus said, 'I am the living bread that came down from heaven. Whoever eats of this bread will live forever; and the bread that I will give for the life of the world is my flesh.'
John 6:51 (NRSV)

Thursday is bread-making day at the Come Back Mission in South Africa. Bread is made from scratch and given to drug-addicted or HIV-positive people in the corrugated tin shacks that spread across the rolling hills outside Soweto. But if our work were just about delivering bread, we could have picked it up at the supermarket.

Many of our mission-team members had never mixed or kneaded dough by hand. Each of us took a turn at hand-sifting the ingredients and kneading the dough while the rest of us sang, recited scripture and prayed aloud for the needs of those to whom the bread would be given. As the dough began to expand in the bowl, we could see what Jesus was talking about when he said the kingdom of heaven is like yeast that a woman took and mixed into a large amount of flour until it worked all through the dough (see Matthew 13:33).

Easily unnoticed and often unseen, the influence of God's love spreads in the world through the hands, hearts and lives of Jesus' followers, affecting the whole. The reign and rule of God grows in this world, Jesus described, like the smallest of all seeds, dropped unnoticed into the soil, until they grow and produce their fruit.

Prayer: *O God, help us to serve others in your name. Amen*

Thought for the day: We who follow Christ are meant to be leaven that changes the world.

Link2Life: *Bake bread for a neighbour in your community.*

James A. Harnish (Florida)

Daily Prayer

Read 1 Thessalonians 5:16–18
Devote yourselves to prayer.
Colossians 4:2 (NIV)

I used to wonder what a day of continuous prayer would be like. I assumed that constant devotion to prayer was only achievable by ordained clergy who have dedicated their lives to the worship of God. However, those of us in the secular world find it a bit daunting. We lead busy lives. With so much to accomplish throughout the day, we rush from one activity to another. Is it any wonder we feel stressed out when the evening comes?

I decided to try to 'pray continually' (1 Thessalonians 5:17), not knowing how to begin, except to repeat formal prayers that I knew. Eventually, I began conversing with God as I would with a good friend. Once we begin to be deliberate about prayer, we come to see God in every part of our lives. Often, prayer requires no words at all. Love and kindness shown to another person are prayer in action.

Prayer: *Dear heavenly Lord, no words can express the depth of our love for you. You fill us with joy as we are born anew. Amen*

Thought for the day: Anything that connects us to God can be a form of prayer.

Terri Meehan (Surrey, England)

Change your Mind

Read Philippians 4:4–8

[The Lord] has sent me to… provide for those who grieve… to bestow on them a crown of beauty instead of ashes, the oil of gladness instead of mourning, and a garment of praise instead of a spirit of despair.
Isaiah 61:1, 3 (NIV)

Many aspects of being in prison make it hard. Nevertheless, whenever I am asked what is most difficult to deal with, the answer readily comes to mind. It is not the cold steel bars, the imposing stone walls or the peril behind them. It is the separation from family, the abandonment by friends and the despairing heart. It is loneliness that truly imprisons.

I will not be released from prison any time soon. However, I am managing some measure of liberation from the prison of loneliness. I've changed what I can—my inward attitude. Doing so has led me to see and experience things differently, to see and experience the goodness that God compassionately offers. Whether we are behind prison walls or the closed doors of our home, loneliness can be the most difficult challenge any of us ever has to face.

Even though we may not be able to change or control our outward circumstances, the Bible tells us we can change our inward attitude toward our situation. Having the 'mind of Christ' (see Philippians 2:5) will change our today… and our tomorrows.

Prayer: *Dear God, whenever and wherever we are lonely, grant us assurance that you are near us. Amen*

Thought for the day: Change starts from within—with help from above.

Charles P. Axe (Pennsylvania)

In Times of Need

Read Daniel 6:4–10

Three times a day [Daniel] got down on his knees and prayed, giving thanks to his God, just as he had done before.
Daniel 6:10 (NIV)

Without warning, I lost my job; and I left on the the day my notice was given. That evening, I adopted my usual habit of Bible reading and prayer, but I was interrupted by a phone call from a friend whom I had emailed earlier with my news. During our conversation, I read from the Bible a phrase that had caught my attention. 'The last thing I expected you to be doing was reading the Bible!' she exclaimed.

Like many people, I suppose, I don't trust God unless I have to. As difficulties have come, though, I've learned not to reject God but to run to God. This has come about through my daily habit of praying and reading the Bible. These actions have deepened my relationship with, and my dependence on, God. I know that I need the habit of listening to God established in my everyday routine so that I will hear God's voice in times of need.

Trust is difficult, especially when our circumstances are hard and our questions aren't answered. Daniel had learned the secret: the habit of daily prayer. That practice offers us help in all our challenges.

Prayer: *Dear God, help us to realise the importance of spending time with you each day. Teach us to love you more in the time we spend together. Help us to love and to trust you in all circumstances. Amen*

Thought for the day: 'Train yourself in godliness' (1 Timothy 4:7, NRSV).

Hilary Allen (Somerset, England)

It's All Good

Read Psalm 104:1–13, 24–30
God saw everything that he had made, and indeed, it was very good.
Genesis 1:31 (NRSV)

In early spring I like going into the damp woods near our home to find the first delicate wildflowers to bloom. There are many different varieties, all blooming and fading during the brief period of warm weather before the trees come into leaf. Exactly why God created these beautiful, short-lived flowers I don't know, but I'm sure there were reasons. God had reasons for the nearby great lakes with their squishy sand, magnificent sand dunes and myriad fish, and reasons for the hot, dry deserts with their lizards and twisty cacti. God even had a reason for creating pesky mosquitoes.

God has created for us great variety—many kinds of beauty, many forms of life. Some life we cannot see; probably some we have not yet discovered. God called every part of creation good.

We can glimpse the reason for some things. We know that green plants produce oxygen for us and absorb the carbon dioxide we breathe out. But we cannot comprehend God's entire, intricate, wonderful design that makes it possible for us to thrive in this world. That doesn't matter. We can still be thankful and respect, cherish and enjoy this beautiful world God made for us.

Prayer: *Thank you, God, for this very good world. Amen*

Thought for the day: Let us care for this amazing planet that God has given us as our home.

Sue Briggs (Michigan)

The Light

Read Ephesians 4:25–32

Stand at the crossroads, and look, and ask for the ancient paths, where the good way lies; and walk in it, and find rest for your souls.
Jeremiah 6:16 (NRSV)

I crossed a busy and dangerous road safely, thanks to new traffic lights. Years ago, before the light was installed, I crossed this road frequently. I often waited a long time to cross and then ran across quickly—a dangerous manoeuvre.

I associated the traffic lights with the Christian life, and I thought of people who act as 'traffic lights' in our life. It is a blessing to count on friends and loved ones who listen, help, counsel and alert us to possible dangers.

In our daily lives, we need help to evaluate our decisions and the possible consequences of our actions. Christian friends can help to guide us as we seek to do God's will. They let us know when to stop, wait or go in a new direction, how to make changes that will help us be better servants; and when to move ahead.

Prayer: *Dear God of hope, we give you thanks for all those who light our path and illumine our lives, as we pray, 'Our Father which art in heaven, Hallowed be thy name. Thy kingdom come. Thy will be done in earth, as it is in heaven. Give us this day our daily bread. And forgive us our debts, as we forgive our debtors. And lead us not into temptation, but deliver us from evil: For thine is the kingdom, and the power, and the glory, for ever. Amen'**

Thought for the day: The journey of life is easier because of God's light shining through friends and family.

Luciria Aguirre Naranjo (Valle del Cauca, Colombia)

* Matthew 6:9–13 (KJV)

Powerful Words

Read Psalm 119:97–105

The word of God is living and active, sharper than any two-edged sword, piercing until it divides soul from spirit, joints from marrow; it is able to judge the thoughts and intentions of the heart.
Hebrews 4:12 (NRSV)

When we needed someone to operate the sound system in our church, one of my relatives offered his services. He warned me, however, 'I will do this for nothing, but please remember that I am an atheist. So don't try and convert me to your faith!' I was pleased with the help he gave. He not only controlled the microphone but also made audio-recordings of the pastor's sermons.

Three months passed. Then one Sunday before the worship service began, I went to pick him up, as he was still serving as our sound-system operator. I was in a hurry to get to worship, and so I greeted him and invited him to follow me to the car. He suddenly stopped me: 'Wait a moment before we leave. We haven't prayed yet!'

Sometimes we fail to acknowledge or we even forget about the power of God's word. When we see those we care about who don't know Christ, we are sad that they don't want to go to church. We may be reluctant to talk to them about God or God's word. However, hearing the word of God has power to change people from within.

Prayer: *Strong God of truth, help us to talk about you more often to our unbelieving relatives. Amen*

Thought for the day: The power of God is at work in people and places we wouldn't expect it to be.

Andrei Pupko (St Petersburg, Russia)

Witnessing Grace

Read Matthew 18:18–22

The Lord said to Paul, 'My grace is sufficient for you, for power is made perfect in weakness.' So, I will boast all the more gladly of my weaknesses, so that the power of Christ may dwell in me.

2 Corinthians 12:9 (NRSV)

Our congregation suffered a horrendous tragedy when a young member, Melanie, who had gone off to college, was brutally murdered. Melanie had been an active member of our worship team. Her family was devastated, as were her friends and fellow students. Our church joined together to create a moving and meaningful candlelight vigil, a memorial service, and later a one-year anniversary service.

After the trial, the young man charged with Melanie's murder was sentenced to life in prison. Melanie's parents were speaking with the press when they heard the sobs from the guilty man's parents. Excusing themselves, Melanie's parents went to the other family and embraced them, both families mourning the loss of a child. What an amazing picture of God's grace!

How often are we unwilling to embrace someone who has wronged us in some trivial way? Yet the parents of a murdered daughter embraced her murderer's parents. That power dwells within all of us when we act with the spirit of grace and Jesus' love.

Prayer: *Gracious God, help us know that your grace is sufficient for us. Help us always to forgive others. Amen*

Thought for the day: Where can I embody God's grace?

Link2Life: *Write a note to someone who's had a loved one die violently.*

Kate Titsworth (Texas)

Give Away Peace

Read John 20:19–23

Jesus said to [his disciples] again, 'Peace be with you. As the Father has sent me, so I send you.'

John 20:21 (NRSV)

As a professional musician, I pass through many busy airports, restaurants and hotels all over the world and see many sad looks and faces that show a weary spirit. It seems as if many people are merely existing.

Everyone has to deal with heartbreaks and challenges. Jesus' words to his disciples, 'Peace be with you!' (John 20:21, NRSV) bring me solace no matter what I face. For me, remembering that Christ offers us peace takes weight from my spirit so that I can live a fuller life.

Some of the people I see in my travels reflect peace in their appearance, their mannerisms and how they treat others. I feel drawn to these people. As a result, no matter where I am in the world, I have tried over these years to give Christ's peace. Giving peace to another person involves more than just words. We can communicate Christ's peace with our smile, the kindness in our eyes, or the touch of a hand when someone is going through tough times—and by doing so we draw others closer to Christ.

As we open our hearts day by day, Christ's peace can fill us so that we are able to share it freely with those we encounter.

Prayer: *Dear Lord, fill us with your love and peace so those we meet will want to know you because of what they see in us. Amen*

Thought for the day: What fills the heart shows in the face.

Chad Jeffers (Tennessee)

Belonging to God

Read 1 John 3:1–5

How great is the love the Father has lavished on us, that we should be called children of God!
1 John 3:1 (NIV)

As I sat beside my husband, a prisoner, in a prison visiting room, I began to notice the people around us. For the first time, I saw these people as brothers, sons, husbands, fathers and, ultimately, children of a forgiving and loving God. They were also men whose identity in society's eyes was a number and a criminal record. Yet aside from the armed guards watching from the corner and the bare, concrete walls surrounding us, the setting could have been any restaurant or family event we might go to. That moment, for me, was the truest picture of how God in rich mercy and grace looks at us.

We may commit vile crimes against God and God's people. And while we must face the legal consequences of such actions, God still sees us through forgiving eyes, with tenderness and love. We are no longer thieves or murderers or liars; we are God's sons and daughters. Very simply, we belong to God; and God never gives up on us.

Prayer: *Dear Father, we praise you that we are called your children, and we thank you for saving and seeing us through Christ's righteousness instead of through our sin. Amen*

Thought for the day: God loves me for who I am, no matter what I have done or will do.

Link2Life: *Become a part of a prison ministry in your area.*

Holly R. Mickler (Florida)

Called to Serve

Read Deuteronomy 15:7–11

Paul said, 'In everything I did, I showed you that by this kind of hard work we must help the weak, remembering the words the Lord Jesus himself said: "It is more blessed to give than to receive." '
Acts 20:35 (NIV)

Following a heart attack, my dad retired in 1984. My parents purchased a mobile home in West Texas. In 1987, they were introduced to Mabel and Elizabeth Claire, a chance meeting that changed their lives. Mabel and Elizabeth had seen the devastation caused by a hurricane and started helping people in the town of Nuevo Progreso, Mexico. Their work consisted of helping to build homes, paying tuition fees for students, helping with medical care and working in a soup kitchen.

Because of these women, my parents heard the Holy Spirit whisper to them to begin building homes for these needy families. Their faith has grown tremendously as a result of answering God's call to serve. My parents believe that God has allowed them many healthy years in retirement. They have a God-directed purpose that keeps them active and has blessed them in many ways as they continue to be faithful to Christ. My parents' view of people has changed. They no longer see stereotypes but think of them as individuals and families whom they deeply love. Who except God could have worked through my dad's health problems to lead my parents to this place and into a growing relationship with Christ?

Prayer: *Dear God, help us to respond to your call to serve wherever we are. Amen*

Thought for the day: God calls us to go where we might never go on our own.

Greg Scott (Hawaii)

PRAYER FOCUS: THOSE REBUILDING AFTER DISASTER

Missing Grace

Read Jonah 2:1–10

Those who cling to worthless idols forfeit the grace that could be theirs.
Jonah 2:8 (NIV)

Have you ever been so upset with another person that your hurt was all you could think about? Recently, I had that experience. As I mechanically went through my daily chores, I ruminated over a wrong that had been done to me. 'How could they do that?' I fumed. 'What were they thinking?' These thoughts swirled around and around in my mind, in an unending loop.

Later that evening at church, I found myself only half-listening to the preacher as I continued to think about how angry I was. Suddenly, in the midst of my fretting and worrying, God gently reminded me of a verse in Jonah which says that if you focus your sights on an idol you will never see God's grace.

An idol is not always a material thing like a sports car or a new TV. Anything that we focus on daily, what we spend our time and our thoughts on, can be an idol. I had wasted my entire day focusing on my emotions as much as if they were a worthless idol. I built an altar and bowed down at the throne of 'I've been hurt and I'm unhappy about it and I'm going to keep feeling bad.' And because my focus was inward, I could not look up and see the grace God was offering, grace to both me and the person who had hurt me. It was time for me to give myself over to God's grace and worship at God's throne instead of my own. Is it time for you to do the same?

Prayer: *Gracious God, help us to not focus on past hurts but to turn our eyes to you so that we can clearly see and accept your grace. Amen*

Thought for the day: What are you focusing on today?

Janna Ramsey (Tennessee)

Privileged to Serve

Read 1 Corinthians 12:12–27

There are varieties of gifts, but the same Spirit; and there are varieties of services, but the same Lord; and there are varieties of activities, but it is the same God who activates all of them in everyone.

1 Corinthians 12:4–6 (NRSV)

I have twin granddaughters who are so different that you would not guess they were even sisters. Though very young, each has distinct characteristics and personality. When they play or work together as a team, each contributes in her own way to the joy and success of whatever they are involved in.

In a similar way, we can see the church functioning well when each of us contributes according to our individual abilities. We can work in harmony with the ministry of serving one another and introducing new people to Christ.

What's more, even when we feel we have limited ability, we are still needed to help fulfil the ministry of the church. The Bible tells us, 'Those parts of the body that seem to be weaker are indispensable, and the parts that we think are less honourable we treat with special honour' (1 Corinthians 12:22, NIV). I am thankful that God gives each of us the privilege to serve and to be included as a useful part of the body of Christ.

Prayer: *Thank you, Lord, for the talents and skills you give us to use in serving others. Amen*

Thought for the day: Today, how will I use the gifts God has given me?

Link2Life: *Make a list of your talents and skills, match them to a ministry in your church and become part of it.*

Walter N. Maris (Missouri)

No Favouritism

Read Leviticus 19:33–34

Do not mistreat foreigners who are living in your land.
Leviticus 19:33 (GNB)

I had been away from home for about six months. One day, I found a shop that sold a kind of ice cream I hadn't had for a long time. I tried to explain what I wanted, but the assistants couldn't understand me. I pointed to the ice cream and tried to say the words in their language, but the women just laughed at me. Eventually, I got what I wanted, but I did not enjoy it because I felt alone in this foreign country.

Then God reminded me of a time a few weeks earlier when I had been in my home country of Australia. I had met a Korean girl who did not speak English well. I knew that she was lonely, and I talked to her a few times, but mostly I avoided her. Having a conversation with someone who didn't speak my language well was difficult. But when I experienced being misunderstood in another country, I wished I'd made more effort to befriend her.

God created the people of all nations and wants us to show no favouritism. God asks us to love the strangers in our midst.

Prayer: *Dear God, thank you for loving the people of all nations. Please help us to see people as you do and to love them unconditionally. Amen*

Thought for the day: God loves people of all races and ethnic groups and tells us to love them too.

Nola Passmore (Queensland, Australia)

Completely Accepted

Read Ephesians 1:1–14

[God] chose us in Christ before the foundation of the world to be holy and blameless before him in love.
Ephesians 1:4 (NRSV)

All my life I have yearned and worked for acceptance. Getting good exam results, working overtime, even accepting unkind treatment from others—I did anything to win approval. I grew up poor, and my dad left us. I felt I wasn't as worthy of love as other people who came from 'normal' families.

Now in my middle years, I understand that even the most confident among us struggle with acceptance. We all need approval for who we are inside. This is why some actors and other public personalities live or die by the whims of a fickle public.

But even if we win applause and trophies, the emptiness we experience can be filled only by God. Why? Only faith in God brings true security. We are accepted; we become whole persons. But this is the work of Christ and not because of anything we have done; we can't be good enough or achieve enough to earn God's acceptance. Out of love and boundless grace, God accepts us.

Regardless of our past, our failures, our sins, God accepts us.

Prayer: *Dear Lord, thank you for accepting each one of us as your own. Help us to realise how much you love us. Help us to stop striving for approval and to find our true worth in you. Amen*

Thought for the day: God accepts you and calls you beloved.

Alicea Jones (Texas)

A Many-Splendoured Thing

Read 1 Corinthians 13:1–13

Because you are precious to me and… I love you.
Isaiah 43:4 (GNB)

'Love is a many-splendoured thing,' sings the old song. What a beautiful way to describe falling in love! Now I switch on the television and the first word I hear is 'love'. But there's something wrong here. I'm watching a tennis match and following the score: 'Fifteen love… 30 love… 40 love… Game.' This means that love equals nothing, love means losing. How can this be? One theory suggests that the word 'love' in tennis was derived from the French word 'l'oeuf', for egg, symbolising a zero. Does this really mean that love means that I have lost?

Jesus has strong words to say about love. He tells us to love our enemies (Matthew 5:44). Not an easy command. And how about loving my neighbour as myself (Matthew 19:19)? It is not always a simple thing to do. To his disciples Jesus gives a new commandment: 'Just as I have loved you, you also should love one another. By this everyone will know that you are my disciples' (John 13:34, NRSV). The good news also comes from Paul in 1 Corinthians 13:1–13, where we learn that of faith, hope and love, it is love that is the greatest.

So love isn't a tennis match. What's the score then? Love means winning every time,

Prayer: *Dear God, help us to focus on the ways we might better use our gifts to express your love, to offer our service, and to do your will. Amen*

Thought for the day: Remember that in all things God works for good for those who love him.

Audrey Mould (Wiltshire, England)

Maps

Read Proverbs 3:5–6

In all your ways acknowledge him, and he will make your paths straight.
Proverbs 3:6 (NIV)

My mum has always liked maps. When she and Dad travelled the world, she was the navigator. When she studies the Bible, she has a map by her side. If she hears that someone is travelling, she gets out her map. The other day, we visited the zoo in Honolulu. On the way, she said that she wished she had a map with her. I assured her that we would get there, but she still wished she had a map.

I like maps too. The map of the world in our hall reminds me of John Wesley's words: 'I look upon all the world as my parish.'

My favourite map for my life is the Bible. But if I'm studying about wandering in the wilderness, it matters not to me where the Sinai desert is. What matters is that I'm lost, and I'm comforted that God is with me. If I'm on the road to Calvary, suffering with Christ, the exact location of that journey doesn't matter. What matters is that I'm with Christ and he's with me. When I travel down any road, I know that God is before me, beside me, behind me and above me. I know this because I have learned about who God is and who I am by studying the Bible.

Prayer: *Dear Lord, help us remember to acknowledge your ways and keep us on your path. Amen*

Thought for the day: If we acknowledge God's constant presence in our lives, God always leads us on the right path.

Beth DeLong (Hawaii)

Highly Favoured

Read Luke 1:26–38

The angel went to [Mary] and said, 'Greetings, you who are highly favoured! The Lord is with you.'
Luke 1:28 (NIV)

I'm single. That wasn't popular to say during my 20s and 30s. While friends made wedding plans and walked down the aisle, I remained alone. My grandmother feared for my future without a husband; friends said I'd be better off married. But I never met a man I could love.

For a while, it bothered me that other women connected with their Mr Right. Was something wrong with me? Or had God simply not led me to the man I was to marry? But I eventually came to cherish another, amazing relationship. Rather than looking for a husband, I committed myself totally to God.

Gabriel called Mary 'highly favoured', and she was—not because she had found a man to marry but because she was chosen by God. And God chooses each of us for a unique role.

Our single or married status in life doesn't carry any weight with God; our relationship with Christ does. All of us can be 'highly favoured' in God's sight by giving ourselves completely to what God asks us to do.

Prayer: *Dear God, thank you for showing us in Mary what really matters to you. Help us to seek you above all others. Amen*

Thought for the day: The only relationship that truly satisfies is relationship with God.

Sherri Langton (Colorado)

Waiting for Wrens

Read Lamentations 3:22–26

The steadfast love of the Lord never ceases… The Lord is good to those who wait for him, to the soul that seeks him.

Lamentations 3:22, 25 (NRSV)

A wren suddenly perched on a bird box hanging in my tree. Through the window, I watched the bird repeatedly poke its head into the hole, jerking its head back and forth. Between looks inside, the bird took several darting glances around the garden. Then, the tiny body disappeared inside. The bird had claimed a home. I was ecstatic.

For four years, I had waited for a bird to inhabit the bird box my dad had lovingly built. Dad had assured me, 'Be patient; they will find it.' Until now, it had hung empty, swinging during snowstorms and swaying with summer breezes, waiting for a bird to take up residence.

Like the birds, I sometimes take a while to find my way home to God. At those times, if I am unable to pray, God hears what is in my heart. When I behave indifferently or even refuse to listen, God doesn't withdraw but instead keeps offering me the choice to do the right thing. And when I need to be reassured and loved, God is always with me to reassure and love me. God doesn't forget us or disappear during the snowstorms or hot summers of our lives. Instead, God is always patient and available, always with us.

Prayer: *Dear God of patience, thank you for your constant love, for always waiting for us—even when we fail to see you or to acknowledge you. Amen*

Thought for the day: No matter how long it takes us to turn to God, we can trust that God will welcome us home.

Mary Beth Oostenbrug (Iowa)

Set Free

Read Luke 23:32–43

People will come from east and west and north and south, and will take their places at the feast in the kingdom of God.
Luke 13:29 (NIV)

As we pulled on to the side of the road with a flat tyre, a man pulled up behind us. As we worked side by side in the mud, it became apparent that he was a believer. When I asked, he told me he was an ex-prisoner and had been released from the prison only 45 minutes earlier. Jesus had set him free in an eternal way twelve years into a 17-year sentence. He vowed to serve those in need because he had neglected the needs of others for so long.

I am glad that we did not know initially that the man helping us was an ex-prisoner, because I fear we would have treated him differently. The last thing he said to us was, 'I thank God the first contacts I had on the outside were believers.'

Twenty centuries ago, another convicted criminal was set free. When Jesus forgave the man hanging on the cross beside him, the man was freed from his past completely. Upon joining Jesus in paradise, I imagine he was welcomed with open arms with no mention of his past. I imagine a time when the thief on the cross, my roadside friend and I will all sit at the marriage supper of the Lamb in robes equally as white as the others (see Revelation 19:7–9).

If Jesus willingly accepted and forgave repenting sinners, so must we.

Prayer: *God of forgiveness and understanding, help us to be watchful for unaccepted people and to show them kindness. Amen*

Thought for the day: Jesus died for all people.

Jonathan Walter (Indiana)

Ageing Gracefully

Read Psalm 71:14–19

For the Son of Man came not to be served but to serve.
Mark 10:45 (NRSV)

I deliver meals to people who are elderly or disabled. The meals I deliver are prepared by volunteers. I am often humbled by the self-lessness and determination of these people. Many of them show the slow, painful movements of age and injury. Some of the volunteers would probably qualify to receive the home-delivered meals themselves. They would not be criticised if they chose the comfort of their own living rooms over the demands of unpaid labour. But they choose 'not to be served but to serve'; and in so doing, they reflect the presence and love of Christ Jesus.

I am reminded that growing older does not mean we must abandon our purpose in life. With God's grace, we are able to continue to serve one another. We do this through actions and prayer and through declaring God's power and love for all generations. We can live with joy and hope, serving others, and with full confidence that Jesus has prepared a perfect and eternal home for us in heaven.

Prayer: *Dear Father, we thank you for the gift of life, both temporal and eternal. Help us to serve you by serving others, as we pray, 'Our Father which art in heaven, Hallowed be thy name. Thy kingdom come. Thy will be done, as in heaven, so in earth. Give us day by day our daily bread. And forgive us our sins; for we also forgive every one that is indebted to us. And lead us not into temptation; but deliver us from evil.'* Amen*

Thought for the day: We never outlive Christ's call to serve others.

Robert Boertien (Oregon)

PRAYER FOCUS: THOSE FACING THE CHALLENGES OF AGEING   117
* Luke 11:2–4 (KJV)

Palm Sunday

Read Matthew 27:45–56

The centurion said, 'Truly this man was God's Son!'
Matthew 27:54 (NRSV)

Today is Palm Sunday, the beginning of Passion week, when we look beyond Jesus' victorious entry into Jerusalem, beyond the crowds and hosannas, to a time of loneliness and isolation. As we reflect on that first Good Friday, the cross reminds us that only through obedience to God did Jesus win the victory.

The celebration of that as-yet-to-come victory began on a palm-covered road. As we look beyond it to the cross, the cheers are not forgotten; the palms laid before Jesus are not in vain. The Son of God is obedient even to the point of death.

Perhaps the signs and wonders that accompanied the death of our Saviour moved the centurion to utter his confession, 'Truly this man was God's Son!' (Matthew 27:54, NRSV). We may be tempted to discount his confession, to value it less, because the centurion saw signs and wonders. But in John 12:32 Jesus says, 'I, when I am lifted up from the earth, will draw all people to myself' (NRSV).

Our scripture passage doesn't tell us what the centurion did after his confession. Did it change his life? Should it have? His story calls us to reflect on our confession of Jesus as Son of God, to ask ourselves, 'How has it changed me?'

Prayer: *Dear Jesus, I confess that you are truly the Son of God. Amen*

Thought for the day: Claiming Jesus as Lord is only the beginning of living our faith.

Alvin B. Deer (Oklahoma)

Stay in Touch

Read John 15:1–11

Jesus said, 'Abide in me as I abide in you. Just as the branch cannot bear fruit by itself unless it abides in the vine, neither can you unless you abide in me.'

John 15:4 (NRSV)

After my church's Palm Sunday service, I brought home two palm-like branches. On a whim, I stuck one of them in a pot that contained a houseplant. I laid the other on a shelf, intending to deal with it later. During the following week as I watered my plants, I was amazed to see that the palm branch in the plant pot was still green. The branch lying on the shelf was yellow and wilted.

'I should have put that palm in the pot, too', I thought, and then I did just that. A few days later, to my surprise, that branch had turned green despite having been on the shelf several days before.

The palm branch in the potted plant was in touch with what it needed for life—soil, water, fertiliser—and so it thrived. The other branch had no such source at first. But when it had soil and water, it too began to take on the signs of life.

This reminds me of our experience as Christians. When we are separated from our source of spiritual life, Christ Jesus, we wither and fade spiritually. But when we stay in touch with our Saviour through Bible study, prayer, devotional reading, serving and fellowship with others, we take on the life Christ has promised us.

Prayer: *Loving God, help us keep in touch with you, the source of our spiritual life. Amen*

Thought for the day: No matter how withered we may look or feel, Christ offers us vibrant life.

Velma G. Warder (Minnesota)

The Spirit's Help

Read Romans 8:18–30

We do not know how to pray as we ought, but [the Holy Spirit] intercedes with sighs too deep for words.
Romans 8:26 (NRSV)

My elderly mother suffers from dementia. She is becoming increasingly dependent, confused and unable to manage independently. She suffers, but the family members who care for her also suffer as we try to meet her increasing needs and help her remain in her home. Caring for a relative with dementia becomes a terrible dilemma when the burden is too heavy and the family must make difficult decisions.

Times such as these make it hard to find the words to express how we feel when we pray. Our struggles seem insurmountable, overwhelming. Sometimes when we do pray, our prayers appear to hit the ceiling and rebound unheard. We can only place our situation (impossible as it seems) in God's hands and take comfort from Paul's words that the Holy Spirit intercedes on our behalf 'with sighs too deep for words'.

When we don't know what to pray or how to pray, we can trust that the Holy Spirit knows our despair and speaks for us in ways we cannot—in 'sighs too deep for words'. We can take comfort that God always knows our sorrow even when we cannot find words to express it.

Prayer: *O Lord, when we do not know how to pray, help us to believe that the Holy Spirit is interceding for us and bringing our needs to you. Amen*

Thought for the day: While words may fail us, the Holy Spirit never does.

Anne Rasmussen (Somerset, England)

Roots of Bitterness

Read Hebrews 12:14–15

Put away from you all bitterness and wrath and anger and wrangling and slander, together with all malice.
Ephesians 4:31 (NRSV)

Working in the garden one day, I knew I had to dig up the weeds that would not allow the flowers to grow. I used several tools to try to pull the weeds out, but to no avail. I became very frustrated. I cried out in anger and resorted to using my hands in trying to pull them out, but the roots were deep.

These weeds reminded me of similar situations in my life. I sensed that bitterness had sent roots deep in my heart. I also realised that only God could remove it so that the seed of God's word planted within me would not die.

After a lengthy process, I managed to remove the weeds from my garden. As happy as I felt about this, I was even happier knowing that when I acknowledge my bitterness and pray about it, God will continually remove the bitterness from my heart. Now the beautiful flowers I see in the garden every morning remind me to be vigilant in keeping my heart free of bitterness.

Prayer: *Dear Lord of the universe, thank you for your infinite love, peace and forgiveness. Amen*

Thought for the day: God's work of transformation goes deep within us.

Eliana Llanos Fuentes (Barranquilla, Colombia)

PRAYER FOCUS: THOSE WHO HARBOUR BITTERNESS

Humility

Read John 13:1–17

Jesus said, 'Now that I, your Lord and Teacher, have washed your feet, you also should wash one another's feet. I have set you an example that you should do as I have done for you.'
John 13:14–15 (NIV)

My friend from another culture would not allow me to handle his shoes as I helped him pack his clothes for travelling because, in his culture, doing so is demeaning. In my culture, it is not dishonourable to touch feet or footwear. Chiropodists and people who repair or sell shoes are not looked down upon. In some parts of the world, however, these and similar occupations are relegated to an 'undesirable' group of people. Understanding this reveals the humility of Christ when he washed the disciples' feet, and it also explains the astonishment of Peter who wanted to stop it.

Even in today's world, some opportunities for service carry the same stigma that foot washing does in my friend's culture. There are still many people, places and situations that 'good' Christians avoid. Perhaps we are prevented by our concern for status and reputation. Maybe our ego or self-image tells us that we are not right for such a humble task. But being like Jesus means disregarding ego and self.

We cannot dismiss Jesus' example by saying it was easy for him because he was the one who could do anything. Instead, we can follow his example as those who would do anything for love's sake.

Prayer: *Thank you, God, for your all-inclusive love and for Jesus' humility as examples of how to relate to others. Amen*

Thought for the day: No task done in love is demeaning.

Kenneth Athon (Indiana)

Suffering Love

Read Matthew 27:11–26

Jesus said, 'Father, forgive them, for they do not know what they are doing.' And they divided up his clothes by casting lots.
Luke 23:34 (NIV)

The young people at our church were acting out some of the events of Holy Week for our Good Friday service. My son, who loves the theatre, had been chosen to portray Jesus. I watched as they acted out the trial, the flogging, the burden of the cross, the stumbling and the torture of Christ's crucifixion and death. Watching my son endure this suffering even as a performance, I was overcome with tears.

This was my son, and I love him! I have many close friends, but I would not ask my son to endure this torture for any one of them, let alone for complete strangers!

But God did. And Jesus suffered. I realised that both God the Father and God the Son endured immense pain that day.

The Bible teaches us that Jesus accepted this suffering. His mercy and sacrifice reach every sinner, every saint, every criminal, every role model, every abuser, every abused—and me. God's love for us and God's desire to reconcile us is that powerful.

How could I not worship such Love?

Prayer: *Amazing, loving Father, you are worthy of all glory, honour and praise. You have suffered immensely for our sake. We accept your love and offer ourselves to be transformed by it. In Christ's name. Amen*

Thought for the day: The family of God includes everyone for whom Jesus died.

Ken Franklin (Michigan)

Mixed Motives

Read Luke 7:1–7

[A centurion] sent some Jewish elders to [Jesus], asking him to come and heal his slave.
Luke 7:3 (NRSV)

I recently noticed something about today's scripture passage that I had not seen before. In other situations where Jesus heals, religious leaders look for ways to trap him (because he healed on the Sabbath or combined it with forgiving sin or for whatever reason). But in this instance, they actually encourage Jesus to heal a person. Why? Self-interest: 'Because he loves our nation and has built our synagogue.' It appears that when Jesus can serve their interests they are all for him. Otherwise, not so much.

As we see often in Luke's Gospel, Jesus heals people whether they 'deserve' it or not. In this case, Jesus overlooks the leaders' wrong motivation and heads toward the centurion's house. With Jesus, life is always about caring for the person.

The changing reactions of those leaders are not unusual. People can quickly change their responses. When Jesus entered Jerusalem on Palm Sunday, cheering crowds surrounded him; days later, people called for his crucifixion. And then Jesus went on to Calvary—not because they deserve it, not because you or I deserve it. Jesus did it because he knew we all need salvation. And Christ is still working on that, one person at a time.

Prayer: *O God, help us to share in your work of bringing healing and salvation to the world, one person at a time. Amen*

Thought for the day: God is changing the world, one person at a time.

Dan G. Johnson (Florida)

Bending the Light

Read Matthew 28:1–10, 16–29

If Christ has not been raised, your faith is futile and you are still in your sins.

1 Corinthians 15:17 (NRSV)

Israel's Roman occupiers had an answer for troublemakers: nail them to a cross! The cross should have been the end of Jesus, scattering his friends and followers. It took amazing courage for the women to come near Jesus' borrowed grave. But what they discovered would turn the world upside down: 'He is not here; for he has risen.'

Resurrection lies outside the realm of ordinary proof. But sometimes proof comes from something neither seen nor understood. For example, Einstein predicted that a large source of gravity could actually 'bend' space, causing light rays to change direction—a theory that was later proved.

So consider Jesus' dispirited disciples and friends, hiding, fearing for their lives. Yet they became a force that changed the world. Something changed them profoundly. We cannot prove or even fully comprehend the resurrection, but we can see its effect as the disciples experienced Jesus alive again.

Without the resurrection, the cross would be only a harsh reminder of human cruelty. But the resurrection 'bends the light' to reveal what has been hidden, showing that even death does not stand in the way of the power of Love.

Prayer: *O God, help us to open ourselves to your transforming love seen in Jesus. Amen*

Thought for the day: Faithful disciples are proof that Christ lives.

F. Richard Garland (Rhode Island)

A Heart Set Free

Read Galatians 4:1–7

You will know the truth, and the truth will set you free.
John 8:32 (NIV)

Last year my dad had his heart checked, and the doctors discovered that six significant arteries were blocked. Surgery was scheduled immediately. The operation, which we were told would take about three hours, took well over five. The surgeon explained that my father had calcification and scar tissue completely surrounding his heart from a previous massive heart attack. Dad's heart was, literally, encased in a shell. The team had to get through that shell before they could repair the damage.

'So,' my wife said to the doctor, 'you set David's heart free.' The repair work was extensive, but my dad's heart could not be mended until it had first been set free.

For me the message was overwhelming, challenging, liberating, redemptive—and clear: at Calvary, Jesus did what's necessary to set our hearts free. Now we can allow him to complete the work of healing.

Prayer: *Thank you for bringing the possibility of a future with hope, Lord. Come into our heart and heal us today. Amen*

Thought for the day: Christ breaks the shell around our heart in order to set us free and heal us.

Derek Maul (Florida)

Only God

Read 1 Corinthians 3:5–9

Neither the one who plants nor the one who waters is anything, but only God who gives the growth.

1 Corinthians 3:7 (NRSV)

Because I am a Christian, I love to share my faith with anyone who will listen, and I will study the Bible with anyone who is interested. I remember a woman who was interested in Christianity and even expressed her desire to become a Christian. She agreed to study the Bible with me to learn more about God. As our study progressed, her convictions grew steadily.

After months of studying God's word and deep reflection on her part, she decided not to become a Christian after all. Though she understood God's love, she wasn't ready to repent of certain sins and embrace total commitment to Christ. The influence of the world was too enticing and she could not let go of it.

Needless to say, I was devastated, and I begged God for an explanation. God answered through 1 Corinthians 3:5–9. I merely planted the word; only God could make it grow in her heart. I did my part, and God remembers that. I finally surrendered her to God, and I pray that someday she will be ready to proclaim Jesus as her Lord.

Prayer: *Dear Father, make us always ready to lead the lost to you. Amen*

Thought for the day: Sharing our faith can prepare hearts to receive God's grace.

Olivia Julius (Sarawak, Malaysia)

God's Steadfast Love

Read Hosea 11:1–11

I am convinced that neither death nor life… nor anything else in all creation, will be able to separate us from the love of God that is in Christ Jesus our Lord.

Romans 8:38–39 (NIV)

Stephen was our determined, defiant son. When he was a toddler, I rescued him from oncoming traffic. When he was a child, I rescued him from snakes and stinging insects. When he was a teenager, I rescued him from a raging fire. But I couldn't rescue Stephen from the bad choices he made as an adult, especially from his choice to leave God out of his decision-making.

My love for Stephen never wavered throughout his 30 years of life. Did I love him any less on the day he died than on the day he was born? No. Because he is my son, he is and always will be a part of me.

Like Stephen with me, I am one of God's defiant children. Regardless of my bad choices and rebellious acts, God doesn't stop loving me. Since I am in Christ Jesus, nothing can separate me from God's love—not angels, rulers, current events or the future; not the powers of this world or the spiritual world; not the heights of ecstasy or the depths of despair. I belong to my Saviour, the One who gave me eternal life. I am forever bound to Christ by the steadfast love of God. Nothing can separate me from the Lord.

Prayer: *Thank you, Saviour, that you love us unconditionally and eternally. Amen*

Thought for the day: Not even our defiance can separate us from God's love.

Jean Matthew Hall (North Carolina)

A New Monkey

Read Psalm 118:19–29

Rejoice in the Lord always. I will say again: Rejoice!
Philippians 4:4 (NIV)

I was surprised to read that scientists recently announced the discovery of a new species of small monkey in the Amazon rain forest. Apparently 1,233 new birds, mammals, reptiles and fish were discovered in 2007 alone. Clearly we still have much to learn and discover about this amazing world God has given us. The same applies to each of us in our Christian journey.

Sadly, especially among young people, I too often seem to hear that Christianity is 'boring'. That is a disturbing and profound sentiment. In my experience, it is also far from true. For me, almost every day the Christian journey brings new discoveries, better understanding, and new insights into the meaning of scripture and the gospel of Jesus Christ.

Perhaps what remains is for each of us to ask ourselves, 'Am I feeling bored and stale in my journey toward heaven?' God offers us new joy each day—no matter what circumstances we encounter. I want to be open every day to this joy that waits all around me to be discovered.

Prayer: *God of all creation, fill us every day with a sense of wonder in the natural world and joy in leading a Christ-filled life. Amen*

Thought for the day: Delighting in the Lord can lead us from boredom to adventure.

Roland Peter Rink (Gauteng, South Africa)

PRAYER FOCUS: SCIENTISTS

Lit by Grace

Read Matthew 6:9–13
Your will be done on earth as it is in heaven.
Matthew 6:10 (NIV)

Each morning, I read my daily devotion and the Bible in Spanish. Spanish is not my first language; but when I read the Bible in Spanish, I pay closer attention. My mind doesn't wander far because simultaneously translating and understanding are difficult for me. At the close of my devotions, I recite the Lord's Prayer in Spanish, focusing each day on a portion of it so that someday I will be able to pray it easily, from my heart, not only from my mind.

Today I was concentrating on the phrase, 'Your will be done on earth as it is in heaven.' I pray the Lord's Prayer every day in English, but I don't always think about the meaning. When I prayed these words today in Spanish, I heard them in a new way—and they said what I needed to hear. I am in a mixed-up time in my life. I am between jobs, and I am not used to being without work. What is God calling me to do? Should I continue in a similar line of work? Should I try something completely new?

Remembering that the prayer 'Your will be done' is sufficient, I have gone about the rest of my day with more peace and security. Despite all the questions I am asking, I am confident that the path ahead will be lit by God's grace.

Prayer: *Gracious Lord, give us confidence that you will guide us into the right decisions as we try to do your will. Amen*

Thought for the day: 'Your will be done' is always a good prayer.

Link2Life: *Read a favourite Bible passage in an unfamiliar translation of the Bible.*

Avis Hoyt-O'Connor (Maryland)

Up to Something

Read Psalm 25:4–10

Show me your ways, O Lord, teach me your paths.
Psalm 25:4 (NIV)

I started knitting some soft, pink bedsocks for my mother-in-law. The knitting began well, but I encountered one or two problems with the pattern and resolved them. But after I had settled back into the rhythm of knitting once more, a problem arose. I puzzled over the pattern, unable to make sense of it. Feeling frustrated, I reluctantly abandoned the project.

'What a shame,' I thought, 'to waste that lovely wool!' I searched the internet for 'Knitting for charity' and found free patterns for knitting clothes for premature babies. Hospitals were desperate for tiny clothes. What a wonderful way to use my pink wool!

I marvelled at how God had been working. I remembered that I had been a premature baby, spending the first six weeks of my life in an incubator. What better way of saying 'thank you' for my life than by helping premature babies? God turned frustration into a means to serve.

God sometimes leads us by surprising means. During frustrating times, we can find comfort in remembering that God has something good in mind for us.

Prayer: *Dear God, please help us use our gifts to glorify you. Amen*

Thought for the day: In frustrating times, remember that God is always up to something.

Elizabeth Moseley (Lancashire, England)

Small Group Questions

Wednesday 5 January

1. What day of the week is typically busiest for you? Why? Do you ever have time for God on that day each week? Why or why not? If so, how do you make time?

2. What people have brought God's touch into your life?

3. What small annoyance or situation 'got to' you recently? Does this same event or situation unsettle you regularly? What might you do to prepare to deal with it differently in the future? If small annoyances don't get to you, what enables you to be like that?

4. In what big event(s) during the last week have you seen God or been aware of God's presence? In what small events?

5. Do you find it easier to feel God's presence in nature or in study, prayer, worship or other religious activities? Why?

6. On a scale of one to ten, with ten being completely satisfied, how would you rate yourself on your day-to-day awareness of God? What evidence can you give for your rating?

Wednesday 12 January

1. What person(s) in your past do you credit with moving you toward relationship with God? What did this person/these persons do?

2. 'Prevenient grace' is God's grace working to draw us toward faith before we're aware of God's desire for relationship with us. Where can you identify prevenient grace in your life?

3. How does your faith community reach out to children? Should you be doing more? How does it reach out to unchurched adults? Should you be doing more?

4. Paul states in 1 Corinthians 3:6: 'I planted the seed, Apollos watered it, but God made it grow.' Relate a time when you 'planted' but didn't see the results of your labour. What helps you to remain faithful in praying and working when you don't see results? Where are you currently waiting to see your efforts bear fruit?

5. Have you ever received a Bible as a gift or reward? If so, what difference did this gift or reward make in your life?

6. Re-read the Thought for the Day. Do you believe what it says? Why or why not?

7. What might be confirmation that we have made a difference in someone's life?

Wednesday 19 January

1. Who is in charge of caring for those in your congregation who are ill? Should caring for those who are ill be the responsibility of paid staff members? What Bible passages support your answer?

2. When was the last time someone took care of you? What did that person do, and why? When did you last help someone?

3. Why do some people find it almost impossible to accept help but find it easy to offer help? Which category do you place yourself in?

4. Carol lists three groups of people she might help: those who are ill, those who are confined, those who are lonely. What other groups need help that your faith community could offer?

5. What group of needy people are you most comfortable with? Least comfortable with?

6. Relate a time when another person's Christian service inspired you to serve.

7. Re-read Matthew 25:31–46. Was the 'goat's' lack of service a result of not wanting to serve or not seeing the need or of something else? Explain your answer. How might the 'goats' change this situation?

Wednesday 26 January

1. What do you know about mental illness from your personal experience? Have your attitudes about it changed because of your experience?

2. Some people believe that Christians can avoid mental and emotional illness if they pray and ask for God's help. Where do you think this idea comes from? Does the Bible connect faith with emotional or mental problems, or are they completely separate issues?

3. How can prayer and medical treatment fit together in bringing healing? Do you think the Bible supports believers' getting medical care?

4. How have you experienced God turning your struggles into something good? Does God always do this? What makes you answer as you do?

5. Describe what you think it means to feel 'hopeless'. Does feeling hopeless only occur when someone suffers from depression? Why or why not?

6. What Bible verses do you recall that help encourage us from despair to joy? Is joy simply a mental attitude, or is it something more? How dependent is it on our circumstances?

Wednesday 2 February

1. What is the longest time you've been away from home? Did you feel lonely during that time? If not, why not? If so, what helped you get through it?

2. Which passage(s) from a New Testament letter seems/seem to be directed specifically to you? What area of your discipleship does this connect with?

3. Jeff compares the Bible to a love letter. In what ways can we say this is true? What other images do we use to describe the Bible? How does each of these shine light on an important characteristic of the Bible? How does each limit what the Bible is?

4. Besides the Bible, creation, Christian friendship and prayer, how do we 'touch Christ's garment' to find healing?

5. In what way(s) does your church reach out to and show appreciation to those serving in the military? Can you think of additional ways?

6. Have you ever written a love letter to Christ? Is it appropriate to do so? Why or why not?

Wednesday 9 February

1. Linda admits her discomfort in approaching Daisy's home on her first visit. Would you feel discomfort about being in a setting such as she describes? Would you admit it?

2. What charity or group of people tugs at your heart and makes you want to give as much as you can? Why does this cause move you?

3. If you were Daisy's niece, how would you feel about what Daisy did with your gift? Why?

4. Linda states, 'Daisy taught me what giving really means.' What *does* giving really mean?

5. What do you think motivates Daisy's generosity? What does Daisy know about giving that some of us may not?

6. What does the Bible say about how we are to give if our resources are abundant? If our resources are meagre?

7. Which do you think is more important to God—the amount we give or our attitude toward giving? Explain your answer.

Wednesday 16 February

1. Have you ever moved from a small town to a big city or vice versa? If so, what did you learn about yourself in the process? What do you think would be the hardest part of such a move?

2. Do you sense that God has a purpose for your living where you do? What is it? If not, how might God use your living situation to teach you or to reach out to people with Christ's love?

3. Brenda placed a plaque in her garden to honour her husband's memory. What other actions do people take to honour someone they love who has died? Which if any have you done? How do such actions help us?

4. What are your neighbours' needs? If you do not know them, how might you find out what they are?

5. Do you pray regularly for your neighbours? Should we all do so? Should we make ways to let them know we are praying for them? Why or why not?

6. How are you working for the good of your city or town? What are its most pressing needs? How is your church working to make your community more like God wants it to be?

7. Do you feel God's presence with us is greater during good times or during troublesome times? When in your day-to-day life do you feel closest to God?

Wednesday 23 February

1. What can we learn about relationship with God from Jesus' model of prayer?

2. List the phrases of the Lord's Prayer. Alongside each, list what it tells us about prayer. For example, what does 'Our Father who art in heaven' say to you about how we are to pray? What does 'hallowed be thy name' say about how we are to pray?

3. Do most people need forgiveness every day? Is it possible to go through an entire day and not do anything for which we need forgiveness?

4. Do you think God's will for us sometimes includes pain and hurt? Why or why not?

5. How have you seen God's grace at work in your or someone else's life in a time of failure?

6. Besides prayer, what other conduits of God's grace are available to us? Which of these do you use most often?

Wednesday 2 March

1. Does your family have someone like Aunt Marion whom everyone goes to with concerns? What draws people to confide in these people rather than in others?

2. Would you feel comfortable praying for or being prayed for by someone in your office or neighbourhood or school? Why or why not?

3. Besides Aunt Marion's practice of copying scripture passages into a journal to apply them to everyday life, what other strategies can we use to do this? What is the most unusual way of using scripture you've encountered?

4. Have you ever tried journaling in response to scripture? If not, why not? If so, what are your journal pages filled with?

5. What amount of faith do you have? When has your faith been the strongest? Why? When the weakest? Why?

6. When have you seen God do the 'impossible' in answer to your prayers?

7. Hebrews 11:6 says that we are to believe that God exists and that God rewards those who seek him. Which of these two requirements do you struggle with most? Why?

8. What objects in your home or other surroundings remind you to pray?

9. How is your faith made visible in your life?

Wednesday 9 March

1. What do you think the manna was?

2. Do you think you'd have tired of the daily miracle of manna and complained about the monotony? Why was the Israelites' complaining so wrong?

3. What can we do to make Lent more joyful and less sacrificial, or should we?

4. What do you do during Communion to focus your mind and heart on its meaning?

5. What would your 'promised land' be like? How would it look? How would people behave?

6. How have you experienced your faith giving you freedom?

7. In a spiritual sense, which means more to you—'the freedom to fail' or 'the faith that could help [you] succeed'? Why?

8. Does your journey of faith and worship more resemble fasting or feasting? To which is Christ calling you now?

9. Are you better at dealing with a sudden crisis or with a long, persistent struggle? Why do you think this is? How did you discover this?

Wednesday 16 March

1. Make a list of specific ideas of how you might brighten another person's day. Compare it with lists of others in the group. Which actions will you take?

2. What obstacles lie in our way when we try to serve with 'love, concern, attention and diligence'? What strategies have you discovered for overcoming these obstacles?

3. Matthew 5:41 says that we should go 'the second mile', doing more than is required. Is this your pattern? How could doing this open a door to talking about our faith?

4. How does this meditation make you feel—happy, hopeful, guilty, tired or something else? Why might it make anyone feel those responses?

5. How do the attitude and actions described in this meditation reflect God's ways of dealing with us? Where has God done more than the minimum in your life this year? This week?

6. What is your community of faith doing to 'invest love, concern, attention, and diligence' in your local area? Outside your local area?

7. Name some of 'God's principles' that, if applied in our lives, would 'allow God's grace to be revealed in and through us'.

Wednesday 23 March

1. How can spiritual activities be part of keeping our minds alert? How can we combine physical and spiritual exercise?

2. Do you feel comfortable offering advice about practical, everyday matters? What determines whether you are willing to listen to someone who offers advice?

3. How do you feel about offering spiritual advice? Should we approach giving practical and spiritual advice differently? If so, why and in what ways?

4. Proverbs 25:11–12 says that a word spoken appropriately is like 'apples of gold in a setting of silver'. When has following someone's advice about a spiritual matter turned out badly for you? When has doing so turned out well?

5. If you were marooned on a desert island without a Bible or a pastor, whom would you want to have with you, and why?

6. When has God's work within you become obvious? What can we do to encourage ourselves when we can't discern God's work in us or in someone we care about?

7. Did you, like Diane, find her father's comment helpful? Why or why not?

8. What signs have you seen that the scriptures have become a part of you?

Wednesday 30 March

1. What do you do regularly to 'train yourself in godliness'?

2. Have you ever had to fire someone or tell people their job was disappearing? If so, how did you handle it? What would be a Christian way to deliver such news?

3. Would you have responded as Hilary did if you were fired? Why or why not?

4. What scripture passages might you quote in a note to Hilary? Could quoting scripture to someone in difficulty be the wrong way to respond? Why or why not?

5. How have you made deposits in a 'spiritual bank account' that you drew on later?

6. Do you read your Bible every day? Do most of your friends know this? How?

7. Do Bible reading and prayer have to be daily to be effective? If so, why? If not, where do we get the idea that they must or should be?

8. How does having 'the habit of listening to God established in [our] everyday routine' help us to 'hear God's voice in times of need'?

9. What do you think Hilary means by 'reject God' and 'run to God'? When have you done either of these?

Wednesday 6 April

1. Have you ever been on a short-term mission? If so, how did it affect you? If not, where would you be willing to go, and why? Where and with whom would you never want to volunteer, and why?

2. Describe 'a God-directed purpose' that you have witnessed in someone's life. How was that person changed or affected by serving God?

3. How have you been stereotyped in your life? How did it feel? Did it limit you or affect your life negatively?

4. When has God transformed your attitude toward a person or group? Did it happen because you prayed for the change, or did God do it without your approval or co-operation, at least at first?

5. When has the Holy Spirit 'whispered' to you? How has God nudged you to serve in a new and different way?

6. Do you see God operating in our lives in the active way that Greg describes?

7. What does this meditation say to you about dealing with prejudiced people? Should Christians work to end bigotry? What Bible passages support your answer?

8. What unexpected or unplanned event or encounter has affected your spiritual life positively?

Wednesday 13 April

1. Does your family take for granted that members will go to college, play a musical instrument, have a bad temper or do other things? What does your family 'believe in'? (For example, hard work, honesty, community service, saving for a rainy day, and so on.)

2. Does your family expect that children will marry and have children? How do you know what your family thinks about this?

3. Is there someone like Sherri in your family? How can we support family members who do not live in traditional situations?

4. How can our expectations for others and ourselves help us and make our lives better? How can they limit us or become a burden?

5. Is it possible for any of us to know God's specific will for another person? If so, in what ways? If not, why not?

6. How does your relationship with God sustain you when human relationships fail you? What do you do to nurture your relationship with God?

7. How are relationship with God and relationship with another person different? How are they the same?

8. How comfortable are you with viewing yourself as the bride of Christ? How would you feel about writing him a love letter?

Wednesday 20 April

1. 'I don't need to go to church. Being out in nature is my worship.' What is true in statements such as that? How are such pronouncements inadequate as expressions of faith?

2. When has an 'un-religious' activity become, for you, a place to meet God? What often turns your thoughts to God and re-creates you? Are these the same thing?

3. What stubborn spiritual and relationship 'weeds' have you struggled over a long time to remove? How is your garden growing today? What new weeds have sprung up recently?

4. Read aloud Hebrews 12:14–15. According to this passage, how can harbouring bitterness affect us and those around us? What does God want for us instead?

5. How/when have you seen bitterness poison someone's life? What strategies can we use to keep bitterness from taking root in us?

6. Realistically, can we 'pursue peace' with everyone? Are bitterness and holding grudges ever acceptable in Christians? Why do you answer as you do?

7. When you have felt deeply rooted bitterness, what experience and/or scripture helped you to remove that bitterness?

8. Do you think it is possible for someone truly to praise and worship God if they feel bitterness toward someone else or some issue? How so? What does the Bible say about this?

9. What do you believe are possible solutions for avoiding bitterness in your life? Describe a process to remove bitterness from our life. Are the two (avoiding bitterness and removing bitterness) the same? Why or why not?

Wednesday 27 April

1. Did your parents consider you rebellious or compliant? Were they right? How has this perception shaped your relationship with God and your image of God? In what way(s) are we all rebellious children in God's eyes?

2. Do you believe that God loves defiant children exactly as much as compliant ones? More than compliant ones? Why would we even ask these questions?

3. For whom have you been concerned and prayed for over a long period of time? What can we do to sustain hope when God doesn't seem to be answering our prayers?

4. What makes you feel separated from God's love? In such times, what can we do to reconnect with God?

5. How might the past cause us to feel separated from God's love? How could the future cause us to feel that, since it's not even here yet?

6. Which word or phrase from today's Bible reading got your attention or connected to your life at the moment? What wisdom does the scripture passage offer you?

7. Jean says that nothing can separate us from God, but some would contend that we can separate ourselves from God. Which is true? What does the Bible say about it?

Bible Reading Resources Pack

A pack of resources and ideas to help to promote Bible reading in your church is available from BRF. The pack, which will be of use at any time during the year (but especially for Bible Sunday in October), includes sample readings from BRF's Bible reading notes and The People's Bible Commentary, a sermon outline, an all-age sketch, a children's activity, information about BRF's ministry and much more.

Unless you specify the month in which you would like the pack sent, we will send it immediately on receipt of your order. We greatly appreciate your donations towards the cost of producing the pack (without them we would not be able to make the pack available) and we welcome your comments about the contents of the pack and your ideas for future ones.

This coupon should be sent to:
BRF, 15 The Chambers, Vineyard, Abingdon OX14 3FE

Name..

Address ....

....Postcode..

Telephone ....

Email...

Please send me...................................Bible Reading Resources Pack(s).

Please send the pack now/ in ....(month).

I enclose a donation for £ .... towards the cost of the pack.

BRF is a Registered Charity

Subscriptions

The Upper Room is published in January, May and September.

Individual subscriptions

The subscription rate for orders for 4 or fewer copies includes postage and packing: THE UPPER ROOM annual individual subscription   £13.80

Church subscriptions

Orders for 5 copies or more, sent to ONE address, are post free:
THE UPPER ROOM annual church subscription   £10.80

Please do not send payment with order for a church subscription. We will send an invoice with your first order.

Please note that the annual billing period for church subscriptions runs from 1 May to 30 April.

Copies of the notes may also be obtained from Christian bookshops.

Single copies of *The Upper Room* will cost £3.60. Prices valid until 30 April 2012.

Individual Subscriptions

☐ I would like to take out a subscription myself (complete your name and address details only once)

☐ I would like to give a gift subscription (please complete both name and address sections below)

Your name..

Your address..

....Postcode...

Gift subscription name..

Gift subscription address..

....Postcode...

Gift message (20 words max)..

....

Please send *The Upper Room* beginning with the May 2011 / September 2011 / January 2012 issue: (delete as applicable)

THE UPPER ROOM ☐ £13.80

Please complete the payment details below and send, with appropriate payment, to: BRF, 15 The Chambers, Vineyard, Abingdon OX14 3FE

Total enclosed £.......... (cheques should be made payable to 'BRF')

Payment by ☐ cheque ☐ postal order ☐ Visa ☐ Mastercard ☐ Switch

Card no:																			

Expires: ☐☐☐☐   Security code: ☐☐☐

Issue no (Switch): ☐☐☐☐

Signature (essential if paying by credit/Switch card) ....

☐ Please do not send me further information about BRF publications

☐ Please send me a Bible reading resources pack to encourage Bible reading in my church

BRF is a Registered Charity

UR0111

Church Subscriptions

☐ Please send me ...... copies of *The Upper Room* May 2011 / September 2011 / January 2012 issue (delete as applicable)

Name...

Address ....

....Postcode..

Telephone ....

Email...

Please send this completed form to:
BRF, 15 The Chambers, Vineyard, Abingdon OX14 3FE

Please do not send payment with this order. We will send an invoice with your first order.

Christian bookshops: All good Christian bookshops stock BRF publications. For your nearest stockist, please contact BRF.

Telephone: The BRF office is open between 09.15 and 17.30. To place your order, telephone 01865 319700; fax 01865 319701.

Web: Visit www.brf.org.uk

☐ Please send me a Bible reading resources pack to encourage Bible reading in my church

BRF is a Registered Charity

UR0111

Jesus Christ—the Alpha & the Omega

Bible readings and reflections for Lent and Easter

Nigel G. Wright

As we pass through the weeks of Lent, our gaze is drawn ineluctably to the Son of God. The crucified Christ fills our gaze as we move closer to Easter, but in order to grasp more fully the scope and significance of his supreme sacrifice, we need to embrace and believe in the whole Christ, Alpha to Omega, rather than focusing only on isolated aspects of his life, such as his teaching or his example—or even his death and resurrection.

There are two journeys to make in this book. The first takes us on an extended exploration of the person and work of Jesus Christ, from the Word present before creation to the Messiah reigning in glory at the end of time. The second journey is one of devotion and discipleship through the events of Holy Week, a journey made in the light of the earlier exploration and enriched by all that we have learned as a result.

ISBN 978 1 84101 704 4   £7.99
To order a copy of this book, please turn to the order form on page 157.

The Promise of Easter

30 reflections for the season of Lent

Fleur Dorrell

'During Lent we are accompanying Christ in a unique way; on a journey that will lead to his death entirely for our sake... Although we are spared all of his agony, it is a time for us to pause and reflect, to pray and, above all, stay very close to Jesus.'

This book considers six themes particularly relevant to the weeks before Easter: holiness, relationship, forgiveness, sacrifice, hope and love. While God's message is for all time, during Lent we are called in a special way to follow him, take up our cross, and enter into the mysteries of Christ's suffering. Most of all, we are asked to show the world pure love, as Jesus did in the sacrifice of his own self for our salvation.

The Promise of Easter also contains creative spiritual exercises and suggestions for art images to aid reflection.

ISBN 978 1 84101 788 4   £4.99
To order a copy of this book, please turn to the order form on page 157.

The Challenge of Caring

Bible-related reflections

Alexine Crawford

First published as *Never Too Old to Grow*, this new edition of a popular BRF title explores, in a series of reflections, aspects of caring and being cared for. Alexine Crawford draws on her own years of looking after her mother as well as the experiences of friends in similar circumstances. Her moving and insightful stories suggest how, despite the often exhausting practicalities of the caring role, there can be a way through to a place of peace and healing, wholeness and joy.

ISBN 978 1 84101 748 8   £7.99
To order a copy of this book, please turn to the order form on page 157.

Prayer

Steps to a deeper relationship

Henry French

This book is about how to embark on the path of prayer, the way that will lead you closer and closer to the heart of God if you follow it faithfully and patiently. Grounded in Scripture, each chapter is filled with wise advice, plus exercises to build confidence not only in intercession, but also meditative prayer and journal-keeping. The aim is always to show how making space for prayer is not only an essential spiritual discipline but a source of deep joy. The book concludes with a further section of helpful ideas and suggestions to put into practice what you have learned.

ISBN 978 1 84101 861 4   £6.99

To order a copy of this book, please turn to the order form on page 157.

Come and See

Learning from the life of Peter

Stephen Cottrell

When we look at the life of Peter, fisherman, disciple, leader of the Church, we find somebody who responded wholeheartedly to the call to 'come and see'. Come and meet Jesus, come and follow him, come and find your life being transformed. This book focuses on Peter, not because he is the best-known of Jesus' friends, nor the most loyal, but because he shows us what being a disciple of Jesus is actually like. Like us, he takes a step of faith and then flounders, and needs the saving touch of God to continue becoming the person he was created to be.

Come and See is also designed to help you begin to develop a pattern of Bible reading, reflection and prayer. Twenty-eight readings, arranged in four sections, offer short passages from the story of Peter, plus comment and questions for personal response or group discussion.

ISBN 978 1 84101 843 0   £5.99   *(available Feb 2011)*
To order a copy of this book, please turn to the order form on page 157.

Celebrating the King James Version

Devotional readings from the classic translation

Rachel Boulding

This book of Bible readings and reflections has been published as part of the celebrations for the 400th anniversary of a classic Bible translation, first published in 1611 yet still widely used and loved around the world today. The King James Version (also known as the Authorised Version) was first published to provide a dignified, authoritative translation for public worship and private prayer, and for centuries it remained the most important Protestant translation into English.

Rachel Boulding's short, insightful devotional readings are drawn from across the King James Version and are written to help the reader reflect on the richness of the language and what it says to us today about faith in God. They can be used for daily reflections, as a bedside book or simply for a fuller appreciation of different parts of the Bible. The King James Version is used as a living book, which speaks to us now. The book concludes with an afterword by Dr Alison Shell of University College, London, on the cultural and historical significance of this most enduring of Bible translations.

ISBN 978 1 84101 757 0   £9.99
To order a copy of this book, please turn to the order form on page 157.

ORDERFORM

REF	TITLE	PRICE	QTY	TOTAL
704 4	Jesus Christ—the Alpha & the Omega	£7.99		
788 4	The Promise of Easter	£4.99		
748 8	The Challenge of Caring	£7.99		
861 4	Prayer	£6.99		
843 0	Come and See	£5.99		
757 0	Celebrating the King James Version	£9.99		

POSTAGE AND PACKING CHARGES				
Order value	UK	Europe	Surface	Air Mail
£7.00 & under	£1.25	£3.00	£3.50	£5.50
£7.10–£30.00	£2.25	£5.50	£6.50	£10.00
Over £30.00	FREE	prices on request		

Postage and packing	
Donation	
TOTAL	

Name _____ Account Number _____

Address _____

_____ Postcode _____

Telephone Number_____

Email _____

Payment by: ❑ Cheque ❑ Mastercard ❑ Visa ❑ Postal Order ❑ Maestro

Card no ▯▯▯▯ ▯▯▯▯ ▯▯▯▯ ▯▯▯▯ ▯▯▯

Valid from ▯▯▯▯   Expires ▯▯▯▯   Issue no. ▯▯▯

Security code* ▯▯▯   *Last 3 digits on the reverse of the card.
ESSENTIAL IN ORDER TO PROCESS YOUR ORDER   Shaded boxes for Maestro use only

Signature _____ Date _____

All orders must be accompanied by the appropriate payment.

Please send your completed order form to:
BRF, 15 The Chambers, Vineyard, Abingdon OX14 3FE
Tel. 01865 319700 / Fax. 01865 319701 Email: enquiries@brf.org.uk

❑ Please send me further information about BRF publications.

Available from your local Christian bookshop.   BRF is a Registered Charity

About
brf:

BRF is a registered charity and also a limited company, and has been in existence since 1922. Through all that we do—producing resources, providing training, working face-to-face with adults and children, and via the web—we work to resource individuals and church communities in their Christian discipleship through the Bible, prayer and worship.

Our Barnabas children's team works with primary schools and churches to help children under 11, and the adults who work with them, to explore Christianity creatively and to bring the Bible alive.

To find out more about BRF and its core activities and ministries, visit:

www.brf.org.uk
www.brfonline.org.uk
www.barnabasinschools.org.uk
www.barnabasinchurches.org.uk
www.messychurch.org.uk
www.foundations21.org.uk

If you have any questions about BRF and our work, please email us at

enquiries@brf.org.uk

enter